GLOBALVIEWPOINTS

Mixed Marriage

Other Books of Related Interest:

At Issue Series

Gay Marriage

Polygamy

Global Viewpoints Series

Civil Liberties

Opposing Viewpoints Series

Multiracial America

Religious Liberty

GLOBALVIEWPOINTS

Mixed Marriage

Margaret Haerens, Book Editor

GREENHAVEN PRESS
A part of Gale, Cengage Learning

GALE
CENGAGE Learning·

Farmington Hills, Mich • San Francisco • New York • Waterville, Maine
Meriden, Conn • Mason, Ohio • Chicago

Elizabeth Des Chenes, *Director, Content Strategy*
Cynthia Sanner, *Publisher*
Douglas Dentino, *Manager, New Product*

© 2014 Greenhaven Press, a part of Gale, Cengage Learning

WCN: 01-100-101

Gale and Greenhaven Press are registered trademarks used herein under license.

For more information, contact:
Greenhaven Press
27500 Drake Rd.
Farmington Hills, MI 48331-3535
Or you can visit our Internet site at gale.cengage.com

For product information and technology assistance, contact us at

Gale Customer Support, 1-800-877-4253
For permission to use material from this text or product, submit all requests online at www.cengage.com/permissions

Further permissions questions can be emailed to permissionrequest@cengage.com

Articles in Greenhaven Press anthologies are often edited for length to meet page requirements. In addition, original titles of these works are changed to clearly present the main thesis and to explicitly indicate the author's opinion. Every effort is made to ensure that Greenhaven Press accurately reflects the original intent of the authors. Every effort has been made to trace the owners of copyrighted material.

Cover image © bikeriderlondon/Shutterstock.com.

LIBRARY OF CONGRESS CATALOGING-IN-PUBLICATION DATA

Mixed marriage / Margaret Haerens, book editor.
    pages cm. -- (Global viewpoints)
    Includes bibliographical references and index.
    ISBN 978-0-7377-6266-2 (hardcover) -- ISBN 978-0-7377-6442-0 (pbk.)
    1. Interracial marriage. I. Haerens, Margaret.
    HQ1031.M59 2014
    306.84'6--dc23

                                                    2013034607

Printed in the United States of America
1 2 3 4 5   18 17 16 15 14

Contents

Foreword   13

Introduction   16

Chapter 1: Trends in Mixed Marriage

1. The **United States** Has Become More   23
   Accepting of Interracial Marriage
   J. Brooks Spector

In recent years, the United States has undergone an impressive cultural shift that has torn down many racial barriers. Evidence of this evolution can be found in statistics showing the rate of interracial marriage at an all-time high. A key factor in this trend is the steady flow of Asian and Hispanic immigrants coming into the United States and expanding the diversity of American communities.

2. Interracial Marriages in **England** Are Common   32
   George Alagiah

In England, mixed-race couples are a common sight and mixed-race children make up one of the fastest-growing demographic groups in the country. Most of these children will be born into stable, middle-class families. Mixed-race communities have a long history in Britain.

3. South Asians in **North America** Are More   41
   Open to Mixed Unions
   David Lepeska

The number of South Asians across North America who are marrying across racial, religious, and ethnic barriers continues to increase. According to statistics, these unions are often more successful than marriages between men and women of the same ethnic community.

4. The South Asian Community in **England**   52
   Sees a Rise in Mixed Marriages
   Roz Euan-Smith

In recent years, there has been a rise in interracial and interethnic relationships in the British South Asian community. There is still resistance to this trend, mainly from nationalistic groups in the United Kingdom and traditional South Asian families, who view mixed marriages as a threat to their cultural and religious values.

5. In Mideast, Interfaith Couples Travel   57
to **Cyprus** to Wed
Associated Press

A growing number of interfaith couples from Lebanon and Israel are traveling to Cyprus to marry. This trend has become popular because civil marriages do not exist in Lebanon and Israel, and marriage is controlled by religious authorities who refuse to marry interfaith couples. Cyprus caters to such couples, making it easy and affordable for them to travel and arrange the marriage ceremony.

6. **Toronto** Is the Mixed-Marriage Capital   63
of Canada
Jan Wong

The thriving city of Toronto was a pioneer in mixed marriages and continues to be a haven for mixed-race couples. One key reason is that immigrants are welcomed in the city and assimilate quickly and relatively easily. This diversity has been beneficial for the economic and cultural life of the city.

Periodical and Internet Sources Bibliography   70

Chapter 2: Factors That Influence the Prevalence of Mixed Marriage

1. **Malaysian** Mixed Marriages Are Common   72
and Accepted in Multicultural Society
M. Rajah

The Malaysian information minister ignited a controversy when he stated that divorce rates were higher in mixed marriages and that young people should think twice before marrying someone outside of their religious, ethnic, or racial group. Malaysia is a multicultural nation with a long history of mixed marriages. The states of Sarawak and Sabah are especially tolerant of such unions.

2. **Japanese** Women Are Influenced by the Media   78
to Prefer Western Men
Rick Wallace

Mixed marriages in Japan are increasing because of the rising numbers of Japanese women, known as *gaisen*, who prefer to marry Western men. Mass media and advertising portray Western men as cool and desirable, which is influencing well-educated Japanese women when it comes to choosing a mate. Another factor may be that Western men represent a break from repressive traditional values that limit the options of Japanese women.

3. Northern **Ireland**'s Acceptance of   85
Catholic-Protestant Marriages Is Based on
Class and Economic Factors
Katrina Lloyd and Gillian Robinson

There are no official statistics on the number of Catholic-Protestant marriages in Northern Ireland. From what information there is on these unions, the couples are younger, better educated, and have higher incomes than marriages involving couples in the same religion. More research is needed on Catholic-Protestant marriages in Northern Ireland.

4. **Indonesia** Has Made Legal Improvements   93
for Mixed Marriages
Nani Afrida

Indonesia passed two laws that make it easier for Indonesian women to marry foreign men and protect children in mixed marriages. Internet websites have also helped inform many mixed couples of their rights and ways to protect themselves under Indonesian law.

5. Interfaith Marriages in the **Philippines** Are   99
Based on Common Heritage
Tingting Cojuangco

Mixed marriages between Christians and Muslims have a long history in the Philippines. Although the religions have very different traditions and customs, they hold similar values. Both religions were brought to the Philippines, and there is a common heritage among all Filipinos that predates the arrival of both.

Periodical and Internet Sources Bibliography   107

Chapter 3: Barriers to Mixed Marriage

1. **India** Is Not Fully Accepting   109
   of Interfaith Marriages
   Vimla Patil

   Indian society as a whole has yet to fully accept marriages of couples from different religions. Mixed marriages spur acrimony in families not only because of the
   religious difference, but also because property, marriage,
   and child custody laws are different for each religious
   group. Mixed unions are more successful when the
   couples are less religious and have supportive families.

2. **Jordanian** Women in Mixed Marriages   116
   Face Legal Discrimination
   Laurent Zecchini

   Jordanian women married to foreigners cannot pass Jordanian nationality to their husbands and children, while
   Jordanian men can. These discriminatory citizenship laws
   are affecting hundreds of thousands of people, many of
   them children who have lived in Jordan their entire lives.
   Political observers suggest that Jordan's troubled relationship to Palestine is at the heart of the country's reluc-
   tance to change the law.

3. **Bosnia and Herzegovina**'s Sectarian Divide   121
   Is Influencing Interfaith Marriage Rates
   Damir Dizdarević

   Rising sectarian tensions and discrimination characterize
   Bosnia and Herzegovina today. It is a shame that the
   country values religion over education and culture and
   threatens those who stand for ethnic tolerance. Mixed
   marriages are not accepted in Bosnian society and are often seen as a threat to powerful religious authorities and
   institutions.

4. Tribal Fighting Frightens **Kenya**'s   131
   "Mixed" Couples
   Shashank Bengali

Intertribal clashes in Kenya have revived long-standing tensions between tribal communities and resistance to intertribal marriages. Intertribal unions are now discouraged, and existing marriages face discrimination, ostracism, and even violence.

5. Intertribal Marriages in **Africa** Are Stigmatized   **136**
Melinda Ozongwu

It has become increasingly common for people in Africa to marry outside their tribes. These marriages often face opposition because of long-standing political or economic conflicts, complicated histories, and stereotypes. Tribal communities often feel betrayed when one of their members marries outside the tribe.

6. **Russia**'s Mixed Marriages Are Endangered by   **141** Cultural and Religious Pressures
Andrei Zolotov Jr.

During the Soviet era, interethnic marriages between Soviet citizens were encouraged and seen as the embodiment of the Soviet ethos. In post-Soviet Russia, a strong religious revival and nationalistic tensions have spurred opposition in many regions to mixed marriages, particularly those between Christians and Muslims.

7. **South Korea** Does Not Support Multicultural   **152** Couples
Steven Borowiec

South Korea is turning a blind eye to the nation's growing for-profit marriage broker business. The government could do a much better job of providing services to the thousands of foreign women who come to the country to marry South Korean men. The country also needs to stop thinking of itself as a uniform culture and accept diversity.

Periodical and Internet Sources Bibliography   **158**

Chapter 4: Some Consequences of Mixed Marriage

1. The Global Prevalence of Interracial Marriage   **160** Will Eventually Blur Racial Distinctions
Matthew Syed

The rate of interracial marriages is increasing gradually worldwide. Some experts predict that this will lead to the obliterations of racial distinctions. Racism, however, is a complex issue based more on psychological factors than genetic ones. That is why racial attitudes are complicated and often difficult to change.

2. Turks with African Ancestors Want Their Existence to Be Felt   168

Ayşe Karabat

There is a significant Afro-Turk population in Turkey, made up of the descendants of African slaves brought to the Ottoman Empire. Over the years, many of these Africans married Turkish citizens, creating a racially and ethnically distinct community that faces discrimination and misconceptions about their racial identity. Some Turks hold suspicious beliefs about Afro-Turks, who find it difficult to be accepted by the larger society.

3. Rising Mixed Marriages Set New Societal Trend   176

Lisa Conrad

The trend of Kuwaiti men marrying foreign women is on the rise. A recent report found that these mixed marriages are more successful than traditional marriages between Kuwaitis. Some observers attribute this to the demanding nature of Kuwaiti culture and the crushing financial expectations placed on young Kuwaiti men and women who marry within their culture. Mixed marriages, many believe, have less societal, familial, and economic pressures.

4. The **United Arab Emirates** Benefits from Mixed Marriages   181

Sultan Al Qassemi

The Grand Mufti of Dubai ignited a firestorm when he suggested that there should be restrictions on citizens of the United Arab Emirates (UAE) marrying foreigners. Such comments ignore the contributions children of mixed marriages have made to the country. Diversity and tolerance are key strengths of the UAE, and discrimination against mixed marriage betrays the country's values.

5. Mixed Couples in **Croatia** and   186
   Bosnia and Herzegovina Face Ethnic
   Intolerance and Discrimination
   Barbara Matejcic

   Mixed marriages are stigmatized in Bosnia and Herzegovina. Bosnian and Croatians are separated by ethnic
   hostility and intolerance. Since the war in Bosnia, the
   number of mixed marriages between both communities
   has plummeted, even in historically tolerant, multiethnic
   cities. Government authorities stoke opposition to mixed
   marriages because they are viewed as a threat to nationalistic movements.

6. **Serbia**'s Surge in Mixed Marriages   197
   Is Reviving Dying Villages
   Zoran Maksimovic

   Mixed marriages between Serbian men and Albanian
   women are becoming more common in remote Albanian
   villages. A scarcity of marriageable Serbian women in
   these villages has forced villagers to reconsider their hos-
   tilities toward Albanians and welcome the influx of young
   brides. These mixed unions are today celebrated for reviving dying villages and ensuring the survival of family
   farms.

Periodical and Internet Sources Bibliography   205

For Further Discussion   206

Organizations to Contact   208

Bibliography of Books   214

Index   217

Foreword

> "The problems of all of humanity can
> only be solved by all of humanity."
> —Swiss author Friedrich Dürrenmatt

Global interdependence has become an undeniable reality. Mass media and technology have increased worldwide access to information and created a society of global citizens. Understanding and navigating this global community is a challenge, requiring a high degree of information literacy and a new level of learning sophistication.

Building on the success of its flagship series, Opposing Viewpoints, Greenhaven Press has created the Global Viewpoints series to examine a broad range of current, often controversial topics of worldwide importance from a variety of international perspectives. Providing students and other readers with the information they need to explore global connections and think critically about worldwide implications, each Global Viewpoints volume offers a panoramic view of a topic of widespread significance.

Drugs, famine, immigration—a broad, international treatment is essential to do justice to social, environmental, health, and political issues such as these. Junior high, high school, and early college students, as well as general readers, can all use Global Viewpoints anthologies to discern the complexities relating to each issue. Readers will be able to examine unique national perspectives while, at the same time, appreciating the interconnectedness that global priorities bring to all nations and cultures.

Material in each volume is selected from a diverse range of sources, including journals, magazines, newspapers, nonfiction books, speeches, government documents, pamphlets, organization newsletters, and position papers. Global Viewpoints is truly global, with material drawn primarily from international sources available in English and secondarily from US sources with extensive international coverage.

Features of each volume in the Global Viewpoints series include:

- An **annotated table of contents** that provides a brief summary of each essay in the volume, including the name of the country or area covered in the essay.

- An **introduction** specific to the volume topic.

- A **world map** to help readers locate the countries or areas covered in the essays.

- For each viewpoint, an **introduction** that contains notes about the author and source of the viewpoint explains why material from the specific country is being presented, summarizes the main points of the viewpoint, and offers three **guided reading questions** to aid in understanding and comprehension.

- **For further discussion** questions that promote critical thinking by asking the reader to compare and contrast aspects of the viewpoints or draw conclusions about perspectives and arguments.

- A worldwide list of **organizations to contact** for readers seeking additional information.

- A **periodical bibliography** for each chapter and a **bibliography of books** on the volume topic to aid in further research.

- A comprehensive **subject index** to offer access to people, places, events, and subjects cited in the text, with the countries covered in the viewpoints highlighted.

Global Viewpoints is designed for a broad spectrum of readers who want to learn more about current events, history, political science, government, international relations, economics, environmental science, world cultures, and sociology— students doing research for class assignments or debates, teachers and faculty seeking to supplement course materials, and others wanting to understand current issues better. By presenting how people in various countries perceive the root causes, current consequences, and proposed solutions to worldwide challenges, Global Viewpoints volumes offer readers opportunities to enhance their global awareness and their knowledge of cultures worldwide.

Introduction

"All marriages are mixed marriages."
—Chantal Saperstein

Intermarriage has a long and complicated history. Since men and women began to settle and form communities, marriage outside of one's community was one key way that different tribes, religions, cultures, and races were able to come together and form ties and alliances that would produce tangible benefits. For example, arranged marriages between different political powers could form a strong military and political alliance and protect against common enemies. Marriages between two economically powerful families could consolidate wealth and lead to further financial gain. Conquerors, traders, and explorers could intermarry with local females in lands they conquered or did business in, thereby establishing valuable bonds between them and the community. Intermarriage could lead to the sharing of important technology, techniques, or resources ultimately beneficial to the community. Throughout history in many cultures, the practice of mixed marriage was not only tolerated but also encouraged to facilitate diversity, increased economic and political advantage, and even survival.

However, in other cultures, mixed marriage was not encouraged. Instead, it was treated as a betrayal of community values and punished severely. In these communities, mixed marriage was viewed as a threat to racial, religious, or cultural purity and the prevailing political and economic power structure.

In the United States, mixed marriage has a long and troubled history. Despite America's reputation as a "melting pot" that welcomes people of every race, nationality, tribe, religion, and culture, there has been a strong resistance to mixed marriage in many sectors—particularly interracial marriage between blacks and whites. The introduction and perpetuation of the institution of slavery in the United States also stoked racial resentment and institutionalized racial prejudices.

Legal impediments to interracial marriages were put in place very early on in American history. In 1664 Maryland passed the first British colonial law banning marriages between whites and slaves. The law dictated that any white woman who married a black male slave became a slave herself. It stated: "Be it further enacted by the authority advice and consent aforesaid that whatsoever freeborn woman shall intermarry with any slave from and after the last day of this present Assembly shall serve the master of such slave during the life of her husband, and that the [children] of such freeborn women so married shall be slaves as their fathers were. And be it further enacted that all the [children] of English or other freeborn women that have already married Negroes shall serve the masters of their parents til they be thirty years of age and no longer."

In 1691 the state of Virginia implemented a law that if a settler married a non-white person—an African slave, a person of mixed race, or a Native American—they would be banished from the settlement and faced almost certain death. In 1705 Virginia expanded the policy by imposing large fines on any minister who performed a marriage between a person of color and a white person. In 1865 Mississippi passed a set of rules called the Mississippi Black Code. One of the provisions prohibited African Americans from marrying whites, a law punishable by life imprisonment. Many other states put in place bans on interracial marriage and other antimiscegenation laws, which prohibited sexual relationships between blacks and whites.

However, some states were beginning to rethink their draconian anti-miscegenation laws. The impetus behind these efforts was the abolitionist movement and the trend in some US states to acknowledge the civil rights of African American people. In 1780 Pennsylvania became the first US state to repeal its anti-miscegenation law as part of a movement to grant African Americans equal legal status in the state. In 1843 Massachusetts followed, spurred by the growing protests against slavery in the North and the state's strong abolitionist movement.

Slavery was abolished in 1865 with the passage of the Thirteenth Amendment to the US Constitution, which states that "neither slavery nor involuntary servitude, except as a punishment for crime whereof the party shall have been duly convicted, shall exist within the United States, or any place subject to their jurisdiction." With this amendment and the North's victory in the Civil War, many political and cultural figures hoped that there might be more tolerant times ahead in American race relations. These hopes would not be realized for decades. In 1871 a Missouri congressman, Andrew King, proposed a US constitutional amendment banning all marriage between whites and non-whites in every state. It did not pass and would be introduced twice more without success.

In 1883 the US Supreme Court complicated the matter in *Pace v. Alabama* by ruling that state-level bans on interracial marriage did not violate the US Constitution. The opinion of the court held that the anti-miscegenation laws did not discriminate on the basis of race because they technically applied the same penalties to blacks and whites. *Pace v. Alabama* proved to be an influential case that impacted the mixed marriage debate in the United States for years to come.

Opponents of anti-miscegenation laws in the United States did not give up, continuing to mount legal challenges to such laws. In 1948 they won a huge legal victory. In *Perez v. Sharp*, the California Supreme Court became the first state high court to declare a ban on interracial marriage unconstitutional.

The growing power of the civil rights movement in the United States in the 1950s and 1960s renewed the hopes of Americans working for racial equality and the elimination of racially discriminatory laws, including interracial marriage bans that still existed in many states. In 1967 the US Supreme Court, in *Loving v. Virginia*, overturned all state bans on interracial marriage, ruling that such laws violated the Fourteenth Amendment of the US Constitution.

As Chief Justice Earl Warren wrote in his decision on the case, "The freedom to marry has long been recognized as one of the vital personal rights essential to the orderly pursuit of happiness by free men. . . . To deny this fundamental freedom on so unsupportable a basis as the racial classifications embodied in these statutes, classifications so directly subversive of the principle of equality at the heart of the Fourteenth Amendment, is surely to deprive all the State's citizens of liberty without due process of law. The Fourteenth Amendment requires that the freedom of choice to marry not be restricted by invidious racial discriminations. Under our Constitution, the freedom to marry, or not marry, a person of another race resides with the individual and cannot be infringed by the State."

With *Loving v. Virginia*, the US Supreme Court had removed all legal impediments to interracial marriage in the United States, but it could not remove all cultural and social obstacles. In many parts of the country, interracial marriage is still not widely accepted and interracial couples face discrimination and even violence. With every passing decade, however, this resistance and bigotry is disappearing and mixed marriages of all kinds are becoming more common in the United States.

The authors of the viewpoints in *Global Viewpoints: Mixed Marriage* examine key issues associated with the state of interracial, intercultural, intertribal, and interfaith marriage around the world, including the growing acceptance of mixed marriage in several countries; various factors that influence its pervasiveness; legal, cultural, economic, and religious barriers to intermarriage; and the impact of politics—especially political conflict—on marriage. The viewpoints provide insight into some of the positive consequences of mixed marriage and the challenges mixed couples face.

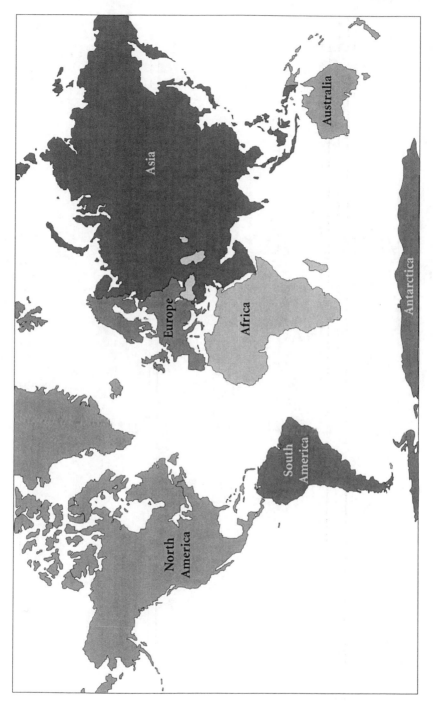

GLOBAL VIEWPOINTS

Trends in Mixed Marriage

The United States Has Become More Accepting of Interracial Marriage

J. Brooks Spector

J. Brooks Spector is a journalist and former US diplomat. In the following viewpoint, he traces the evolution of racial attitudes in the United States toward interracial marriage, noting that more and more Americans are accepting the practice. A 2012 Pew Research Center study confirms this broad trend, reporting that there are not only more interracial marriages in the United States, but also the demographic of multiracial Americans is growing quickly and will become more than half the population of the country by 2050. Spector speculates on the effect this trend will have on politics and political representation in the United States in the future.

As you read, consider the following questions:

1. What is the "one drop" rule, according to Spector?
2. According to a 2012 Pew Research Center study, what percentage of all current American marriages are interracial?
3. What percentage of Americans does the Pew Research Center study report is in favor of interracial marriage?

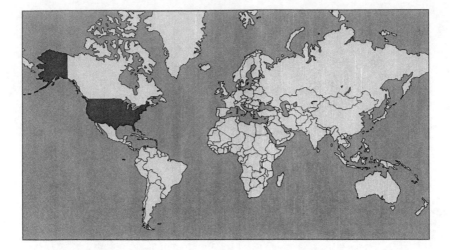

Thirty-five years ago, while exploring one of the Smithsonian museums of Washington, this writer looked at an ex-
hibition that explored the complex way racial differences had
been portrayed in colonial America—in the Spanish and Portuguese colonies as well as the British and Dutch ones. From
among all the items in this problematic but fascinating exhibi-
tion, one item stopped me in my tracks.

It was a beautifully embellished chart, painted on a square
wooden panel, covered with Baroque flourishes. It had eight
squares along its horizontal and eight along the vertical axes,
thereby giving 64 individual squares in total. Each square con-
tained a picture of a man and a woman—or the two of them
with a child. At the upper left, the family was very European
in appearance, while at the bottom right-hand corner, the
three figures were virtually black. But in the other 62 blocks,
the gradations described a visual dictionary of the whole racial typology of Latin America—mestizo, mulatto, quadroon,
octoroon—and on into dizzyingly minute distinctions and
categories. It was the world of sixteenth-century law and sociology in miniature, illuminated through a table of human
physical variety.

The True Message

And of course, the legal status of the tiny people in each one of those 64 blocks was slightly different—from top-of-the-heap on down to much worse. But a further, more subliminal message of the chart, of course, was that—even back in the sixteenth century—there had already been a substantial mixing of the gene pool, bringing together Europeans, Asians, Amerindians and Africans for generations. And so it has been wherever and whenever the descendants of those original small groups of hunter-gatherers left Africa to populate the rest of the earth some 70,000 years ago.

Of course, men (and it has usually been the men) have often tried to enforce prohibitions of intimacy between the different groups of people that evolved out of those ancient migrations—usually justifying these values on the basis of some incidental differences in the width of the bridge of the nose or skin colour (in association with man-made cultural traditions, languages and religions). Out of such a goal came apartheid in South Africa and Jim Crow segregation in the US. By the time such prohibitions had come to have legal sanction in South Africa, of course, whole populations of people had come into being, drawn upon the world's gene pool. And the African American populations of the New World had come to hold genetic material from the whole world in their cell nuclei as well.

Racial Attitudes in the United States and South Africa

From the eighteenth century onward in the new United States, legal prohibitions increasingly made black-white interracial marriages (although certainly not sex) almost impossible under the presumptions of the so-called "one drop" rule: one drop of "African American blood" from children from such unions effectively [made them] African American as well. But as Eusebius McKaiser noted in his recent column in the *New*

York Times, South Africa's populations of mixed racial heritage have generally had more complex relationships with the vagaries and idiocies of racial categorisation than has historically been true in the United States.

South Africa's premier social satirist, Pieter-Dirk Uys, had an entire cabaret routine that used to consist of simply reading from the parliamentary record the official notifications of people who had successfully petitioned the government to allow them to change their racial classification. He would solemnly read that so many Chinese became Indian, so many coloured people became Indian, so many whites had magically turned into Indians, Malays or coloured South Africans. It would bring the house down every time.

Changing Attitudes on Race Relations

Meanwhile, a real sea change has been slowly moving through American society for the past several generations in which people increasingly are jumping the racial fence there as well—or just plain ignoring it. A brand-new Pew Research Center study documents just how impressive this change has been.

According to the study released on 16 February [2012], interracial marriages in the US have climbed to 4.8 million—a new high of 1 in 12 marriages. Besides changing attitudes, a key contributing element in this evolving pattern seems to be coming from the steady flow of new Asian and Hispanic immigrants that is considerably expanding the pool (and the diversity) of prospective spouses. Simultaneously, black Americans are now substantially more likely than before to marry whites as well.

Sociologist Daniel Lichter at Cornell University argues that based on the results of this survey, "The rise in interracial marriage indicates that race relations have improved over the past quarter century. Mixed-race children have blurred America's color line. They often interact with others on either

Banning Interracial Marriage

In 1967, the United States Supreme Court struck down laws in 16 states prohibiting interracial marriages. Fifteen years earlier, 14 other states had also banned interracial marriage but repealed their laws before the 1967 decision.

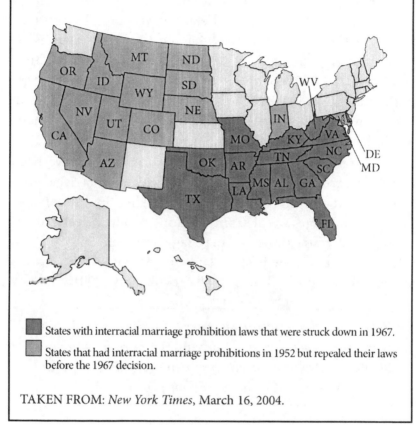

States with interracial marriage prohibition laws that were struck down in 1967.

States that had interracial marriage prohibitions in 1952 but repealed their laws before the 1967 decision.

TAKEN FROM: *New York Times*, March 16, 2004.

side of the racial divide and frequently serve as brokers between friends and family members of different racial backgrounds [although] America still has a long way to go."

A Surprising Picture

The Pew study shows 8.4% of all current American marriages now are interracial, up sharply from 3.2% in 1980. While Hispanics and Asians remained the most likely, as in previous decades, to marry someone of a different race, somewhat surprisingly, the largest increase in share in the past four years has occurred among blacks, a population that historically has been the most segregated. Also, America's western states with their large populations of Asian and Hispanic immigrants, were among the most likely to have couples who "marry out"—at 20%. The small, rural state of Vermont, by contrast, had a "marry out" rate of only 4%. Of course the state is almost entirely populated by white Americans so maybe they don't meet too many people who don't look like what they see in the mirror. Overall, more than 15% of all new marriages in 2010 were interracial in America—not quite the picture many would have expected before this study was released.

Such results also track other Pew surveys that have been measuring greater public acceptance of mixed marriage since 1967. In that year, the Supreme Court, taking the case of *Loving v. Virginia* on appeal from the lower courts, declared racially based restrictions on marriage were unconstitutional (although the last such state law—in Alabama—long overlooked and unenforced, was finally revoked in 2000).

Taken together, multiracial Americans (beyond all those who carry genetic variety from history, of course) are one of the country's fastest-growing demographic groups and they now represent about 9 million people.

In its decision, the court had decided on "whether a statutory scheme adopted by the State of Virginia to prevent marriages between persons solely on the basis of racial classifications violates the Equal Protection and Due Process Clauses of the Fourteenth Amendment. For reasons which seem to us to reflect the central meaning of those constitutional commands, we conclude that these statutes cannot stand consistently with the Fourteenth Amendment." Now, isn't *Loving v. Virginia* the most appropriately named court case ever?

According to Pew's new data, some 83% of Americans now agree it is "all right for blacks and whites to date each other," up sharply from only 48% back in 1987. Meanwhile, nearly two-thirds said "it would be fine" if a family member were to marry outside their own race. Minorities, young adults, the higher educated and those living in western or northeast states also agreed mixed marriages represent a change for the better for society. On this issue, 61% of 18–29-year-olds agreed, in contrast to only 28% of those 65 and above.

Changing Demographics

Taken together, multiracial Americans (beyond all those who carry genetic variety from history, of course) are one of the country's fastest-growing demographic groups and they now represent about 9 million people. The Census Bureau now estimates that multiracial people, blacks, Hispanics and Asians will—collectively—equal more than half the total population of the country by 2050.

Beginning with the [Barack] Obama election of 2008, will all future presidential tickets now strive to include individuals that engage with the increasingly interwoven racial texture of American families, thereby capturing the changing demographics of the US?

According to the Pew report, more than a quarter of all Hispanics and Asians who married in 2010 had a spouse of a different race, while over 17% of blacks and almost one in 10 whites did as well. When one stops and contemplates those numbers, they sound suspiciously like the family tree of the current residents of the White House, along with many other American families.

Finally, among all of the 275,500 new interracial marriages concluded in 2010, 43% were white-Hispanic, 14.4% were white-Asian, 11.9% were white-black, and the remainder came from other, more interesting—or unusual—combinations. For example, when the writer last lived in the Washington area, one of his younger daughter's best friends was a child whose parents were Iranian and Korean. Such is the growing power of social mixing and the growing diversity of the American population as a whole.

Paul Taylor, director of Pew's Social & Demographic Trends project, comments, "In the past century, intermarriage has evolved from being illegal, to be a taboo and then to be merely unusual. And with each passing year, it becomes less unusual. That says a lot about the state of race relations. Behaviors have changed and attitudes have changed. . . . For younger Americans, racial and ethnic diversity are a part of their lives."

Political Implications

Now, this being an election year in America and thus a period when everything can be observed through the lens of electoral contests, the writer cannot help but wonder what effect such trends will have on American politics in the future. Beginning with the [Barack] Obama election of 2008, will all future presidential tickets now strive to include individuals that engage with the increasingly interwoven racial texture of American families, thereby capturing the changing demographics of the US? After all, for decades, successful electoral politics in New York City, the great melting pot as it was labelled, always aimed for a potent mix of candidates for major elected offices, each drawn from among all the major hyphenated American and voter groups of the city—Jews, blacks, Hispanics, Irish- and Italian-Americans—and eventually Asian-Americans as well.

It is more than a little ironic, of course, that in light of the *Loving* decision, the state with the highest rate of white-black married couples in America is now nowhere else than Virginia—the very same state that 150 years ago was the core of the confederacy in a revolt against the federal union that was predicated upon preserving African American slavery.

Interracial Marriages in England Are Common

George Alagiah

George Alagiah is a British journalist. In the following viewpoint, he reflects on the prevalence of mixed-race people in Britain, pointing out that many of the nation's most famous and successful citizens are products of mixed-race marriages. Alagiah recalls that only a few decades ago mixed-race relationships were often met with prejudice and rejection, but today social attitudes have changed to the point where such relationships are barely noticed. He also notes that mixed marriages were never banned in Britain.

As you read, consider the following questions:

1. According to British census experts, how many mixed-race people will there be in Britain by 2020?
2. What does Alagiah say that mixed-race children born to white women and black service members stationed in Britain during World War II were called?
3. What percentage of Britain's population is mixed race today, according to the author?

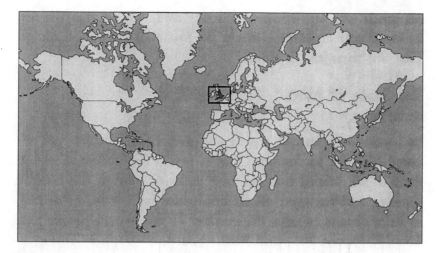

It is only when my wife, Frances, and I go back and look at our wedding album that we realise quite what a meeting of cultures our marriage was. Not so much for the two of us but for our parents. My Sri Lankan mum in her red and gold sari, and Mary, my English mother-in-law, in her floral patterned suit—it sort of sums up the journey the two families were making.

The truth is that Frances and I were willfully unconcerned about the challenges that our different heritage and colour might throw our way. Not everyone around us was quite so sanguine. Years after we got married in 1984 we heard about a conversation between Frances's father, Charles, and her grand-father.

"Is this Ala-what's-it educated?" the older man had asked.

"My dear man, that boy is more educated than you and I will ever be," was Charles's reply. It was quite a retort coming from a man who had himself studied at Oxford.

But even Frances's father, who had stuck up for me so elo-quently in public, had felt the need to have a private word with her once we had announced our decision to marry. In his gentle way this country solicitor told Frances that life for us—and our children—might be just that bit more sticky. That was then, this is now.

The State of Mixed-Race Families in Britain

In London—indeed, in any of our great cities—mixed-race relationships are so common that it would be strange to notice them at all. Mixed-race children make up one of the fastest-growing and youngest ethnic minorities in Britain. According to some census experts, the number of mixed-race people will double between 2001 and 2020 when demographers predict it will reach about 1.3m people. Far from being saddled with disadvantage (my father-in-law's instinctive fear), the latest evidence suggests that most of these children are born into more stable, middle-class families than the popular stereotype would suggest.

Mixed-race people number among our most famous and high-achieving citizens—there's Lewis Hamilton, the former Formula One world champion; Leona Lewis, the pop singer; Zadie Smith, the novelist; and Chuka Umunna, the rising star of Labour politics, to name a few. A survey conducted by Cardiff University's school of psychology found that mixed-race people came closest to modern notions of what it takes to be attractive. Think of all those honey-coloured models so favoured by the advertising industry. The professor in charge of the study suggests that those taking part in the survey may have, subliminally, stumbled across what Charles Darwin once called "hybrid vigour".

A Shameful Past

Yet it is not so long ago that to be born mixed race in Britain was to carry a burden of shame and opprobrium. While filming *Mixed Britannia* for BBC Two, I interviewed Connie Ho. She was born in 1921 to a Chinese father and a white, English mother. I met Connie in Limehouse, east London, the original Chinatown, with her great-grandchildren. She remembered vividly how she and other mixed-race children were taken to an upstairs room above a restaurant to be measured by scientists. They recorded the distance between her eyes, the width of her forehead, the colour of her eyes and carried out a host of other pseudo-scientific tests.

This was in the 1930s, the heyday of the eugenicists, and their fascination with mixed-race children was far from benevolent. In fact it was not until the Holocaust laid bare the revolting use that eugenics had been put to in Hitler's Germany that British champions of the flawed science recoiled in horror.

The History of Mixed-Race Communities in Britain

Like most people, I had always assumed that mixed-race communities, with their own defined space and culture, really began only with post-war mass immigration. How wrong I was.

On a cold morning in March I knocked on the door of a mid-terrace building in South Shields. Inside, Abdo Obeiya and Yahia told me about the Yemeni cafes and shops that had once lined the streets near the harbour. Like veterans from a forgotten war, these two men told me how they used to sweat their way through months-long voyages in the underbelly of a steamship, feeding coal to the ever-hungry furnaces. They were stoking the fires of commerce. They were not the first of their kind. Their fathers had done it before them. That would have been in the early 1900s.

Trade and empire—the foundations of British wealth—are the reasons why these men from a desert nation ended up braving the chill winds of winter in far-away Britain. In Cardiff, Hull, Liverpool, Bristol and London the story was the

Resident Population Estimates by Ethnic Group, 2009 (in England)

All ethnic groups	51,809,700
White	45,313,300
Mixed	956,700
Asian or Asian British	3,166,800
Black or black British	1,521,400
Chinese or other ethnic group	851,600

TAKEN FROM: Office of National Statistics, 2010.

same. Young men, spruced up in their shore suits, stepped off the gangway and found fun, companionship and love in the arms of British women.

Facing Racial Prejudice

It was love in a cold climate—and I'm not talking about the weather. The women who took up with these seamen were more often than not cut off from their families. They were accused of being sluts and their children described as lice-ridden half-breeds.

Surrounded by this wall of prejudice and rejection they still managed to build communities of genuine warmth and cohesiveness, truly multicultural before the term had been conceived. In Tiger Bay in Cardiff, Eid al-Fitr, the festival that marks the end of the Ramadan fast, was celebrated by Muslims and Christians alike.

These early mixed-race communities made it up as they went along, unhindered by the rigid political correctness and religious righteousness that would come later. (Some of the older people we spoke to still referred to themselves as "half-caste" or "coloured", though both terms began to be seen as offensive in the late 1980s.) Norman and Maureen Kaier—both of them the products of Yemeni/English unions—told me how their mothers kept a separate pan for frying bacon.

No sooner had their Muslim fathers stepped out of the front door than the delicious aroma of an English breakfast wafted through the terraces. Everyone knew what was going on and nobody made a big deal of it.

The road to social acceptance has been a long and rocky one.

Racial Pioneers and Feminists

The determination of these women to fall in love with the man of their choice was an act of feminism, even though most of them would never have thought of describing it as such. What they lacked in conventional education and status they made up for with sheer guts and heart, no more evident than when they defended their men in the race riots of 1919 (yes, race riots in 1919!) and later.

Women like Emily Ah Foo were pioneers. Under some arcane interpretation of legislation designed to intern Germans in Britain during the First World War, Emily, a white English woman, was forced to renounce her birthright because she married a Chinese seamen, Stanley Ah Foo. She was deemed an alien in her own land.

The injustice and humiliation still rankle with her mixed-race daughters Lynne and Doreen, now in their eighties. "I think it's disgusting, really," Lynne told me. "She was born and bred in England. She was English, white. So why should she, because she married an alien, have to give up everything?" You might have thought the decades would dim her anger—far from it.

Social Acceptance

The road to social acceptance has been a long and rocky one. In the 1940s, the children born to white women and black GIs [servicemen] stationed in Britain were described as "war casualties" here, and in America one congressman called them "the offspring of the scum of the British Isles". These affairs, forged in the uncertainty of war, produced a thousand or so babies. As it happens, my brother-in-law, Tony Martin, was one of them. Like so many of the "brown babies", as they were called, he was handed to Barnardo's [a British orphanage], his mother unwilling to face the public distaste she would have had to endure if she tried to raise him herself.

Tony was one of the lucky ones. He was fostered by a family, the Tabors, in the village of Balsham, near Cambridge, and whenever we have talked about his early life he has always remembered it as a period of undiluted joy. I knew he had met his natural mother but it was not until I interviewed him for the programme that I discovered there was an occasion when she asked him to live with her. But he was happy where he was. One can only imagine the heartache of this young woman.

As for Tony, he's as British as they come. On our last holiday to Sri Lanka together he insisted on Marmite and toast for breakfast while the rest of us enjoyed the local fare—buffalo milk curd and kitul pani.

What I've realised while shooting *Mixed Britannia* is that it is not really a history of race but about Britishness—that elusive quality we all understand instinctively but find so difficult to encapsulate in words. This country was subject to the same prejudices and pressures as the United States and Germany yet we avoided the worst excesses of bogus science or political extremism.

There were calls for anti-miscegenation laws, but we never banned mixed marriages. True, there were ghettos, but we never accepted outright segregation. There were—and are—plenty of racists, but they have never been allowed to gain the foothold they did elsewhere. Somehow we have muddled through to where we are today, a country largely at ease with its rainbow people. Given what is happening elsewhere that is something to be proud of.

Love and Race

- Mixed-race people make up about 1.1% of Britain's population, according to analysis of official figures by Lucinda Platt, professor of sociology at the Institute of Education, part of London University. That proportion is likely to grow because 3% of under-16s are of mixed heritage and 9% of children live in households of mixed ethnicity. Overall, one in five children belongs to an ethnic minority.

- Intermarriage is most common among black men. Nearly half (48%) of men with a Caribbean heritage who are in a relationship have a partner of a different race. The same is true of one in five black African men, one in 10 Indian men and women, and 39% of Chinese women (though only 17% of Chinese men). The lowest rates of interethnic relationship were among the white population, at 3% for men and 4% for women.

- Intermarriage rates are lowest among ethnic groups that are geographically concentrated. Pakistanis have an interethnic relationship rate of 7% for men and 5% for women; Bangladeshis have rates of 8% and 6% respectively.

- Muslim women are the least likely to be in a relationship with a man of a different faith, with only 3% doing so, followed by Sikh, Hindu and Christian women at 7–9% and Jewish women at 30%. Among men, 5% of Christians, 10% of Hindus, Sikhs and Muslims, and a third of Jewish men are in interfaith relationships.

- In the past 14 years the proportion of children with one parent of Caribbean heritage and one white parent has risen from 39% to 49%. Among the Indian population it has increased from 3% to 11%, for Pakistanis from 1% to 4%, and for Chinese from 15% to 35%.

South Asians in North America Are More Open to Mixed Unions

David Lepeska

David Lepeska is a writer for Open *magazine. In the following viewpoint, he reports that South Asians across North America are marrying non-Asians at much higher rates than two decades ago. In fact, these marriages are proving to be more successful in the long run than intra-ethnic unions among South Asians. Lepeska finds that older generations have become more tolerant of mixed marriage, but that Asian males often face more resistance for marrying outside of their ethnicity than women do. Lepeska concludes that challenges to such unions include dealing with cultural differences and facing prejudice from others outside the marriage.*

As you read, consider the following questions:

1. According to census figures, what percentage of Asian American marriages are interracial?

2. What percentage of Asian females in the United States does the author report go for mixed marriage?

3. According to researcher Arpana Inman, what plays a role in dynamics of mixed couples featuring an Indian spouse?

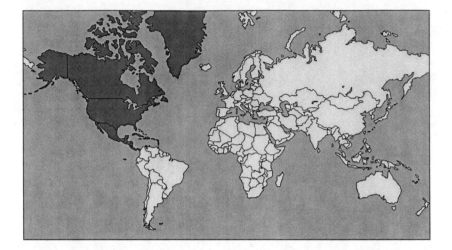

In a recent TV commercial for BharatMatrimony.com, a mother approaches her family in the living room. "He's bringing that Amy," she informs her daughter, husband and mother. "Amy?" asks the grandmother, "*Gori?*" The father expresses grumpy disapproval and buries his head in a magazine. "Please be cool," the mother begs. The ad cuts to a handsome young man sitting across from the father. "Dad, meet Amy," he says. The camera pans left to reveal a pretty young *desi* girl sitting next to him. "*Namaste*, Uncle, I'm Amritha," she says, "My dad's a doc in New York." Everybody smiles and the dark clouds scatter.

A Hopeful Trend

This nearly racist ad sums up the received wisdom on the ideal mate for most Indian American parents, who generally see their children marrying within the community. Yet, South Asians across North America appear to be marrying non–South Asians at much higher rates than two decades ago, as older generations of immigrants come to grips with the American melting pot. "It's definitely increased," says Arpana Inman, professor of sociology and South Asian studies at Lehigh University in Bethlehem, Pennsylvania. She admits that there is limited data on such marriages, particularly from previous decades. Yet, "I think you could safely say that it's doubled."

For centuries, Indians and other South Asians have tended to marry within the same geographic region, religion, socioeconomic status and caste.

What's more, among South Asians, interethnic unions often fare better than intra-ethnic. "*Desi-desi* marriages are more fragile than *desi*-White marriages in the US," says Shaifali Sandhya, a Chicago-based clinical psychologist and the author of *Love Will Follow: Why the Indian Marriage Is Burning.* She cites an excess of parental involvement and the couple's resulting inability to find privacy as possible explanations.

What the Statistics Report

Precise data is very hard to come by, but according to Census Bureau information, less than 1 per cent of all US marriages in the 1970s were interracial or interethnic. Today, the overall number is 15 per cent, and among Asians, it's nearly 29 per cent. Further, a study by Inman found that for Indian females in America, the US-born are more than four times likely to marry white males than women of Indian origin born in India (19 per cent to nearly 4 per cent). Similarly, Indian males born in the US are more than thrice as likely to marry white females than their Indian-born counterparts in America (18.5 per cent to 6 per cent).

Still, it constitutes a defiance of tradition. For centuries, Indians and other South Asians have tended to marry within the same geographic region, religion, socioeconomic status and caste. For many who emigrate to Canada and the US, keeping up matrimonial traditions is one way to avoid cultural dilution as a minority arrival to a country of many peoples. Also, the bias against marrying an 'outsider' is stronger among certain sub-ethnicities and castes, such as Tamil Brahmins. [Detailing traditional views on marriage and their reasons would require an entire book, not to mention an exhaustive and exhausting study. Thus, for brevity, this (viewpoint) will tend to view Indians in North America as a near-monolith.] South Asian parents also view intra-ethnic marriages as a shortcut to finding mates with similar values, and worry that mixed unions could create a distance between first generation parents and their grandchildren, undermining the family unit.

Mixed-Marriage Pioneers

Decades ago, prominent Indian Americans like Zubin Mehta, a Parsi from Bombay who became a leading American orchestra conductor, began blazing a trail. Mehta, the longest-serving lead conductor of the New York Philharmonic, married Canadian soprano Carmen Lasky in 1958. After their divorce, he married American actress Nancy Kovack in 1969.

In more recent years, well-known Indian Americans like Fareed Zakaria have also married people of other ethnicities. But few highlight the changing times better than Anu, a Canadian Bengali based in Ottawa, whose narrative may be representative of the broader experience of Indians in mixed unions. Now a development economist, Anu left Calcutta to study at Cornell University in the 1960s and has lived in Canada for most of her adult life. In 1972, she married a white Canadian man despite the reaction of most of her Bengali friends at the time. "It was extremely uncommon," says Anu. "The people who knew my family were completely scandalised that we'd done this, and they'd ask, 'Did your mother know?' 'Did she approve?'"

Anu admits she came from an exceedingly liberal Calcutta family: "My mother had said to me, 'I'm not going to find you a husband, so you must choose who you want to marry.'" Anu and her first husband divorced after 18 years, but cultural differences played no part in the split. In 2001, she married again, this time a white Jewish man from the US. Today, some of her friends who were scandalised by her first marriage have white sons-in-law. "I've now sort of become part of the furniture," says Anu, laughing at the changed response. "They no longer see me as horrible or a groundbreaker or anything else. In fact, I think Indians have become more accepting."

Growing Acceptance

Jimmy Soni might agree. His parents are from Rajasthan, but he was born in France and moved to the Chicago suburbs as a four-year-old, the eldest of two boys. Now 25 and a mayoral adviser in Washington, DC, Soni has dated mostly white women. "That's just how it happened," he says, "It was never by design." But the reaction has been something of a surprise. "It's kind of affirmed for me how open people can be," he says, speaking of his friends, relatives and parents. "I had prepared all these long speeches that I would give if it became an issue, but I've never had to use them."

Soni says his parents have had more issues with the fact that he *was* dating than *who* he dated. Mainly, they want his future wife to have a similar set of values—emphasis on education, importance of family and respect for elders—and a level of comfort with her family. "I know they were sceptical at first," says Soni. "But as they've met the girls I've dated, maybe they've learned that my radar isn't as bad as they thought it was. They've come to realise that I'm not picking people who have no ability to interact with them, so they've managed to give me the benefit of doubt as a result."

Gender Expectations

Soni's case is something of a surprise to some. Sandhya says that males of Indian origin—particularly the eldest—face stiffer parental resistance on the idea of a mixed union. "Hindu society places a lot of importance on propagation of the fam-

"I'm warning you, Goopta —
these mixed marriages
never work out."

ily line through males," she explains, "So there's greater pressure on first-born males to marry within the community." It's not just Hindu society; only a fifth of Asian males in the US go for mixed marriages, while some 40 per cent of all Asian females do.

Consider this case. An American girl named Cara, a journalist living in the New York area at the time, met a Tamil Brahmin man on a connections website. Their relationship progressed slowly at first, but then became serious, and within a year they had moved in together. Cara soon found that a white American girl was not welcomed too warmly by his family. Once, while riding the subway, he told her of his parents' ranking of girls, from most desirable mate to least. A white girl ranked fifth, tied with dalit, black and Muslim. On a visit to Chennai to attend the wedding of an old friend of his, her reception, at the reception, was icy. 'Every woman aged 40 and above gave me the coldest stare imaginable, a mix of disgust and anger,' she says via email.

Later, she met his parents, and asked his father about his favourite adventure—had he really hiked into Tibet on foot? "Yes," the boyfriend's father responded, full stop. 'If this were a movie,' Cara recalls, 'the silence would have been so deafening you would have heard the clock ticking on the wall.' Their relationship ended after five years, and her Tamil Brahmin boyfriend later married an English girl. 'At least his parents came around and went to the wedding,' says Cara, 'I think by that stage, they were just happy he didn't come home with a boy in tow, announcing he was gay.'

The Case for Women

That's not to say mixed relationships are easy for Indian women. One young Tamil Brahmin woman in the US looked for a husband within her community for years, trying everything from websites like Shadi.com (distinct from Shaadi.com) to family setups. By her early 30s, she'd started dating a white American journalist. They married in Chennai in 2009, and during a recent visit to India, the new wife heard her aunt whisper to a friend, "We couldn't have found a better boy even if we had searched."

Indian mothers typically expect their daughter-in-law to spend a great deal of time with the extended family, cooking and taking care of the family domestically. Janis McClinch, an Irish Catholic woman from Connecticut, has experienced this firsthand. McClinch and her husband Rajive Chaudhry, both architects, split their time between Lexington, Massachusetts, and New Delhi, where they run a boutique guesthouse and spend time with his family.

The fact that all of Rajive's three older brothers married Indian women may have smoothened the way for their marriage, at least from the Chaudhrys' perspective. But it's taken

Janis some time to get used to the stream of friends and relatives constantly flitting in and out of their Delhi home. "Occasionally, I'll have moments when I want to scream," she says. "It's not like I don't want to spend time with all these people, but I do need some downtime."

A Successful Match

Subrata Chakravarty, a longtime business journalist whose father served as Indian ambassador to the United Nations, has had a good many years of downtime with Bess, his American wife of 40 years. They met in the summer of 1968, when he was 21 and a junior at Yale, and she had just graduated from boarding school.

"I had no intention of getting married. . . . I wanted to join the Indian foreign service," remembers Chakravarty, an only son. "I'm pretty sure my mother assumed I would marry someone Indian."

His parents had moved back to India the previous year, when his father took over as governor of Haryana. Chakravarty's guardians in the US at the time were an older couple who had been his parents' neighbours for years. They visited India for his parents' 30th anniversary and told them Subrata may have met a girl he wants to marry. "My parents asked a bunch of questions," says Chakravarty. "And my father said, 'I trust my son's judgment and if this is the girl he wants, then that's fine.'"

He was not yet sure how serious he was about Bess. "I was serious about making a decision: 'You can have foreign service or you can have the girl—you can't have both,'" he recalls telling himself. "I was leaning towards 'I want to have Bess.'"

Bess's family and friends were worried that, since his parents had moved back to India, he might do the same. "She had her family and her friends saying, 'You're getting involved with this guy, his visa will run out at some point and he'll go back home,'" says Chakravarty. In the end, the two of them spoke, and he told her he was indeed serious. "I picked right," he adds. "She showed an incredible amount of courage and willingness to take risks."

The Challenges of Mixed Marriage

For some, the challenges are even greater, yet still not enough to keep them apart. Roy Wadia, originally from Bombay, has lived and worked in the US and Canada for the past 25 years. While working towards his master's in accounting at the University of Georgia in 1989, he met Alan, a Taiwan-born Chinese man. The two fell in love and have been together ever since—they married in 2008 while living in Vancouver, Canada.

Being the eldest son and one-half of an Indian Chinese gay couple in the early 1990s could not have been easy. But Roy says his parents were neither homophobic nor racist. They did, however, expect him to marry a woman. "It was just once that my mother sent me the photo of a friend's daughter in the US to see if I was interested," Wadia recalls. "Once my mother met Alan, however, she just knew, even without my saying it, that we were a couple—it was the way we were together that spelt it all out."

Cultural differences cropped up often in the early years, causing trouble. Even today, his relationship is still a discomfort to some of his friends in Mumbai, where he's living at the moment.

Facing Racism

But many mixed couples recall incidents of subtle and not so subtle racism. One incident stands out for Chakravarty. On the way to a dance for one of Bess's friends in Washington, DC, in 1969, they were pulled over by a cop while Bess was driving. "She said 'We're looking for Georgetown and we're kind of lost,'" he recounts, "He gave her directions, then asked, 'Is this man bothering you?'"

Chakravarty was less upset than he might have been, pointing out that this was a different era in terms of race relations. Anu's experience with discrimination, on the other hand, was more personal, and more acute. She was at a gathering of the family of her first husband, sometime in the late 1970s. "I remember one of my husband's cousins saying, 'Oh, there are too many coloured immigrants moving into our area, I think housing prices will go down.'" Anu recalls. "I said, 'I beg your pardon?' And he said, 'Oh, Anu, we're not talking about you!'"

But a more recent incident may have been the worst. In 2007, Janis and Rajive were leaving a restaurant in Cambridge, Massachusetts, after dinner and a middle-aged white man followed them out. He hurried after their car as they started to drive, opened the driver's side door and closed it again on Rajive's arm.

As such [mixed] marriages have increased, the experiences of such Indian couples have become increasingly diverse, hinging on issues that are not unlike those of more traditional marriages—psychological and emotional factors, privacy, honesty and ability to communicate.

"We pulled away and parked across the street," says Janis, "I was thinking, 'No way are we going to let this guy get away.'" She told their attacker, who had now retreated to his SUV with his wife and two adult daughters, that she was going to call the police. "He drove over the sidewalk, threw a beer bottle at me and said, 'That's what you get for marrying a foreigner!'" says Janis. "And his wife said, '9/11 bitch!'"

Janis and Rajive took the man to court and got a restraining order. Though she was pregnant during the stress of the trial, the incident may have actually brought the two closer. "It broke both of our hearts," she says. "My husband is an amazing human being. He said that it made him realise that people object to the colour of his skin, and it made me so sad."

Race Dynamics

Such incidents are no surprise to Inman, the researcher, who recently studied the dynamics of mixed couples featuring an Indian spouse. She found that ethnicity (and being a minority) often plays a role. "This comes into play in terms of how others perceive the marriage, in both the minority community and the majority community—the stares they receive, the discrimination," she says.

As such marriages have increased, the experiences of such Indian couples have become increasingly diverse, hinging on issues that are not unlike those of more traditional marriages—psychological and emotional factors, privacy, honesty and ability to communicate.

Inman found some predictable clashes of culture. One husband learnt that his wife had never had Santa Claus come to her house when she was a child. "I never considered putting up a Christmas tree would be a discussion," he told the researcher.

Yet, such problems need not undermine or weaken a mixed marriage. Ask Inman. "These marriages are just as healthy as any other marriage," says the professor. "One advantage is that these people are going in with eyes wide open and saying, 'Well, these are differences,' and they deal with them beautifully."

Janis McClinch seems to have done just that. "People ask me what it's like to be married to an Indian," she says. "And I say, well, 'I've never been married to anyone else.... My family just sees how good he is, and that I'm happy, and that's all that matters.'"

The South Asian Community in England Sees a Rise in Mixed Marriages

Roz Euan-Smith

Roz Euan-Smith is a journalist. In the following viewpoint, she contends that mixed marriages involving South Asians in England are more common than they were years ago, when such unions were regarded as taboo. Euan-Smith finds that there are more resources for these couples and more acceptance from their families and communities. However, there can be difficulties that come into play when older generations get involved because they are concerned that interethnic relations will dilute their culture, faith, and values. She argues that the only way to really change racial opinions is to find a way for different groups to mix and learn about other traditions and values.

As you read, consider the following questions:

1. Why does the author say that some Hindu parents shave their child's head?

2. What is the British National Party (BNP)?

3. Where does the author say one can find forums and discussion groups that support extreme attitudes about race and national identity?

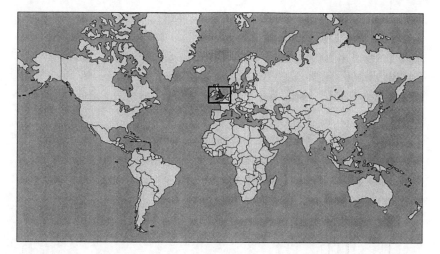

Walking through any of the popular areas in central London these days, you wouldn't bat an eye lid if you saw families or couples with mixed ethnic backgrounds. Although these relationships are widely accepted by our society a quick Google search brings up advice on how to make interracial marriages work, interracial dating sites and forums discussing the pros and cons of these relationships.

There are many articles accessible online with tips on how to get along best if your partner is from another culture. The advice is very similar to general marriage advice, namely respect each other and each other's right to be different. Sharing similar values is more important than being from the same ethnic group.

Generational Expectations

The difficulties appear when older generations and family members are entered into the equation. Every parent has expectations of their children, and some fear that marrying someone from a different racial community will take their children away from their own culture.

Anil Patel, 34, of London believes that a lot of the older generation's negative attitudes are due to a fear that these relationships will cause dilution of their faith, values and religion. Born in the UK [United Kingdom] to Indian parents, he has had several relationships with women from other cultures. After finishing university his sister decided to move in with her white boyfriend, who her parents knew nothing about at the time.

Anil helped his sister break the news to her parents. "It was really tense in the house. She went upstairs to tell my dad, and was gone ages. I went up to see everything was ok, she was crying and my dad was hugging her."

His mother had concerns about the relationship, but "everything changed when they met her boyfriend" and the family now get on very well together.

Every parent has expectations of their children, and some fear that marrying someone from a different racial community will take their children away from their own culture.

A Positive Experience

Alex Marsh, 27, of Tunbridge Wells had a similarly positive experience with the family of his British-born Indian wife, Jayna. The couple met at university in Manchester and had their first child in March this year [2011].

Although Alex refused to let Jayna's parents shave Sophia's head, which according to Hindu tradition removes undesirable elements from the child's past lives, he is happy for his child to take part in other aspects of Indian culture. Jayna wants her daughter to grow up knowing some Gujurati, particularly family words such as "Aunty", and to celebrate Diwali and Holi.

In general, there is a rise in interracial relationships and marriages amongst the British South Asian community. You are seeing such relationships practiced much more openly than in the past, especially by Brit-Asian women dating non-Asian men. It is now common to see them dating white British men or other nationalities. Also, Brit-Asian men with Afro-Caribbean [women] is also a trend.

Threads of Resistance

Some people are not so accepting of interracial relationships as these examples.

Traditional and orthodox British Asian families would see interracial relationships as something completely unacceptable or a phase, especially, for men dating non-Asian women. Parents in this situation would not expect the relationship to last, and therefore, eventually would expect the man to marry someone from within his own community.

There have been cases where some British Asian men have even lived away from home, had children with the non-Asian woman, and then some years later decided to leave the relationship and revert back to marrying a woman from their own culture, frequently from abroad, such as India, Pakistan or Bangladesh. A practice not so common in women from the British Asian community.

Organized Opposition

The rise of the British National Party (BNP), an extreme right-wing political group, in recent years is a clear indication of extreme attitudes about race and national identity becoming more mainstream.

Online you can find a wide array of forums and discussion groups that support these ideas.

On such a site there is a thread with the title: "Interracial marriage should be banned—reasons for and against." The user listed three reasons against, namely "Whites are a world minority", "Race mixing is against nature", and "For Christians, race mixing is outlawed in the 10 commandments." They didn't make any positive comments about interracial marriage and ended their post with the statement:

"It is against nature, it is against God, it is against good sense and instinct. That's why interracial sex is wrong."

Thankfully other users of the forum unanimously disagreed with the reasons put forward. However, these attitudes are certainly out there, and should not be swept under the carpet.

Fighting Ignorance

The only way to change people's opinions is for them to get to know people from the group they are prejudiced against. Obviously this isn't easy, especially as many people hold stereotypes and prejudices without realizing it.

Older generations may be frightened of their children moving away from the traditions of their homeland, but surely this is a natural part of migration and living in a foreign culture. Is it either fair or realistic to expect people who have grown up in the UK to follow rules dictated by a culture that they haven't experienced in the same way?

In Mideast, Interfaith Couples Travel to Cyprus to Wed

Associated Press

The Associated Press is a leading international news agency. In the following viewpoint, the author examines the popularity of the small island of Cyprus as a site for interfaith couples from Lebanon and Israel to marry. Because civil marriage does not exist in the Middle East and no religious authority will perform interfaith ceremonies, couples from different faiths are forced to travel abroad to marry. Cyprus is close to both countries, offers affordable travel packages and marriage services, and provides a romantic backdrop for such an event.

As you read, consider the following questions:

1. How far is Cyprus from Lebanon, according to the author?

2. How many couples from Israel does the author say were married in Cyprus in 2008?

3. In what year did the Israeli Supreme Court rule that common-law marriages would have many of the same rights and benefits as those in religiously sanctioned unions?

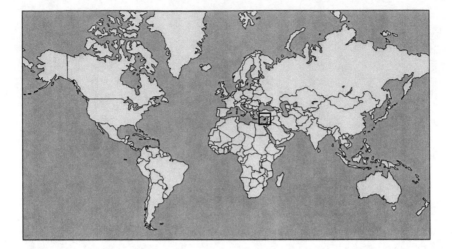

The two couples had never met each other, and probably never would. They had come from opposite sides of a border between longtime enemies.

But Elie Wakim and Nada Ghamloush from Lebanon, and Dimitri Stafeev and Olga Zaytseva from Israel, had a problem in common: Belonging to different religions, neither couple could get married in their home country, and had to fly to the Mediterranean island of Cyprus to tie the knot.

A Marriage Haven

In the Middle East, civil marriage doesn't exist and no religious authority will perform an interfaith wedding. Lebanon and Israel are different in that they recognize civil marriages as long as they're performed abroad, and the closest venue abroad is Cyprus, 150 miles from Lebanon and 230 miles from Israel.

So this little island, which claims to be the birthplace of Aphrodite, the Greek goddess of love, has made mixed marriages something of an industry. Its municipalities charge around $415 for express processing and $190 for others, while travel agencies in both Lebanon and Israel offer packages including travel, luxury hotel, marriage fees and flowers for the bride.

Last year [2008], by Cyprus government count, 523 couples from Lebanon and 1,533 from Israel were married here.

An Interfaith Love Story

Wakim, 39, and Ghamloush, 33, met at work, fell in love and decided to marry. Their problem was he's a Maronite Christian, she's a Baha'i. So Cyprus was their best bet.

Their wedding at City Hall in Nicosia, the capital, was quick and unadorned. A photocopier next to the Wedding Room whirred and creaked as municipal workers handled paperwork. The groom slipped outside for a quick smoke in the parking lot.

So this little island [of Cyprus], which claims to be the birthplace of Aphrodite, the Greek goddess of love, has made mixed marriages something of an industry.

Then the marriage officer arrived, recited his lines in English, and the couple exchanged vows. It was over in 10 minutes.

They snapped a few photos of themselves on the steps of City Hall, then hurried off to finish the paperwork. They were catching a 40-minute flight back to Beirut that evening.

Another Couple in Love

Many other couples stay on to honeymoon on the island, a sunny, laid-back escape from their high-stress lives back home at the center of the Mideast conflict. One such couple is Dimitri Stafeev and Olga Zaytseva, two 29-year-olds of Russian descent who live in a town near Jerusalem.

He's Jewish, she's a Russian Orthodox Christian, so they couldn't marry in Israel unless one of them converted to the

Early Cyprus History

Human settlement on Cyprus stretches back nearly eight millennia and by 3700 BC, the island was a crossroads between East and West. The island fell successively under Assyrian, Egyptian, Persian, Greek, and Roman domination. For 800 years, beginning in 364 AD, Cyprus was ruled by Byzantium. After brief possession by King Richard I (the Lionheart) of England during the Crusades, the island came under Frankish control in the late 12th century. It was ceded to the Venetian Republic in 1489 and conquered by the Ottoman Turks in 1571. The Ottomans applied the millet system to Cyprus, which allowed religious authorities to govern their own non-Muslim minorities. This system reinforced the position of the Orthodox Church and the cohesion of the ethnic Greek population. Most of the Turks who settled on the island during the three centuries of Ottoman rule remained when control of Cyprus—although not sovereignty—was ceded to Great Britain in 1878. Many, however, left for Turkey during the 1920s. The island was annexed formally by the United Kingdom in 1914 at the outbreak of World War I and became a crown colony in 1925.

Cyprus gained its independence from the United Kingdom and established a constitutional republic in 1960, after an anti-British campaign by the Greek Cypriot EOKA (National Organisation of Cypriot Fighters), a guerrilla group that desired political union, or enosis, with Greece. Archbishop Makarios, a charismatic religious and political leader, was elected president.

"Background Notes: Cyprus,"
US Department of State, 2012.

other's faith. Converting to Judaism is a long process of study and ritual, and can be especially difficult for immigrants from the former Soviet Union who may have grown up with no religious education.

Stafeev and Zaytseva were married this month [October 2009] near the seaside city of Larnaca, in a century-old mansion renovated by the municipality with carpets and antique furniture to serve as a suitably romantic backdrop.

No Civil Unions

In Israel, the Orthodox rabbis who control marriage and divorce argue that their strict definition of Jewishness—it passes only through the mother—is vital to preserve the unity of a long-persecuted people, and to spare the offspring of mixed marriages from inheriting similar problems when their time comes to marry.

Clerics are just as firm in Lebanon, whose Muslim and Christian populations subdivide into 18 officially recognized religious groups.

"For us, a person who has civil marriage is like a person who is committing adultery," Father Joseph Abdul-Sater, a Maronite Catholic priest and religious judge, told the Associated Press. "The marriage is the sacrament while civil marriage is a contract, and for that reason it is considered cohabitation."

Mohammed Dali Balta, a Sunni Muslim judge, said in an interview that if human beings are allowed to write marriage laws, rather than live by religiously sanctified Muslim law, "they can one day legalize marriage between homosexuals."

Common Ground

The Israeli and Lebanese couples who marry in Cyprus tend to feel bitter and discriminated against, and while they may consider each other enemies, they would probably find much to agree on as far as marriage law is concerned.

"Who is ruling the country? In a way, it's the religious parties," said Wakim, 39, the Lebanese groom. "Not separating the church from government from the beginning . . . this is the biggest problem."

Ghamloush, his 33-year-old bride, said Lebanon, with so many religious groups, badly needs civil marriage. "Because if you respect your partner, you shouldn't expect him to change his religion for you."

Stafeev, who works in construction in Israel, said people's religion should be their own affair. "Israel is a democratic state," he said. "Everyone should have the will and the right to do what they want."

Both Lebanon and Israel have champions for change.

A Growing Campaign

Last year a campaign called "All for Civil Marriage in Lebanon" spread through Facebook and became a movement that is trying to legalize civil marriage for those who have no other option, said Basil Abdullah, a Lebanese civil rights activist.

Political rivalries have stymied the effort, he said, but he was optimistic it would eventually succeed.

In Israel, the marriage issue is a political line in the sand that can threaten governments dependent on religious parties for their parliamentary majorities.

Mixed couples in common-law marriages have won some relief from a 2002 Supreme Court ruling granting them the same rights and benefits as those in religiously sanctioned unions, but they still aren't recognized by the state as married unless they go abroad and have a civil marriage.

Irit Rosenblum, a civil rights lawyer who campaigns for civil marriage, says for many couples, equal benefits aren't enough; to be registered by the state as married "is really important mentally for them."

Toronto Is the Mixed-Marriage Capital of Canada

Jan Wong

Jan Wong is a Canadian journalist. In the following viewpoint, she finds the trend of mixed marriages in Toronto to be proof of the city's energy and diversity as well as a welcome change from the past, when there were few visible minorities and ethnicities did not mix outside of their chosen enclaves. Wong credits big corporations with catering to immigrant groups, providing much-needed community outreach to minorities, and putting mentoring programs in place for minority employees. She sees her own mixed-race children as a sign of the future, when ethnic and racial differences will be even less prominent.

As you read, consider the following questions:

1. According to Statistics Canada data, how many Toronto couples are in mixed marriages, legal and common law?

2. How many immigrants from China, India, the Middle East, and Latin America have been recruited by the Royal Bank as personal account managers in the past couple of years, according to Wong?

3. What percentage of the Royal Bank's Toronto-area employees does Wong report are visible minorities?

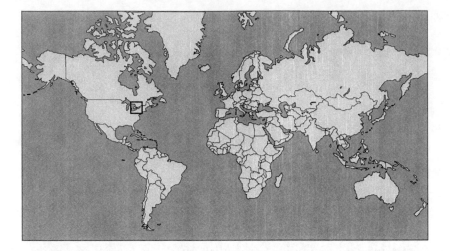

This fall, my husband and I will mark the 34th anniversary of our Chinese-Jewish marriage. Back in 1976, some folks (OK, my parents) fretted it would never last. "Think of the kids! Neither side will accept them," my mother warned. It took 14 years—and the birth of our first child—before she quit running in hysterics from her house whenever my husband dropped by. (I'm not kidding.)

Yet in 2010, not only am I still married, with two fairly acceptable sons, I find myself living in the mixed-marriage capital of Canada. Toronto famously blazed the way for same-sex marriage. Today, it turns out to be a Petri dish for innovative people combos. According to the latest Statistics Canada data, nearly twice as many Toronto couples are in mixed marriages, legal and common law, as the rest of Canadians, 7.1 per cent versus 3.9 per cent. That number covers all existing unions, including dusty old ones like mine.

Toronto's Impressive Diversity

The much more impressive stat is how many young visible minorities are marrying outside their tribes. In what the census bureau calls the Metropolitan Area of Toronto (which includes Pickering and Ajax to the east, Milton and Oakville to the west, and Georgina on the shores of Lake Simcoe to the north), 45 per cent of second-generation immigrants who are married or living common law are doing so with someone of a different race or ethnicity. By the third generation, it spikes to a stunning 68 per cent.

The next time a wedding motorcade honks at you, check out the newlyweds: More often than not, the happy couple will be crossing ethnic boundaries. Until now, Toronto's diversity has been viewed in terms of silos: a Chinatown here, a Tamil enclave there. But true diversity occurs when we interact—and there's nothing more interactive than sex.

Toronto famously blazed the way for same-sex marriage. Today, it turns out to be a Petri dish for innovative people combos.

Our city is so blasé about racial mixing and matching that no one bothered commenting on the ethnicity of [Canadian politician] Adam Giambrone's side dish. Was the secret girlfriend who met him for trysts on his city hall couch Filipino? South American? Who cares? The only time the "R" word was mentioned was in this context: Giambrone exits mayoral race.

A Big Change

Toronto has more couples in mixed unions than anywhere else in the country. Looking at the latest stats, I have to pinch myself.

I was born in Montreal more than half a century ago, and at the time it was Canada's most cosmopolitan city. How cosmopolitan? Let's put it this way: I was the one and only vis min [visible minority] in my church choir. At Montreal West High, a public Anglo school, there were just three non-WASPs [white Anglo-Saxon Protestant] in my entire grade: a black girl, a Jewish boy and myself. As my graduation prom neared,

Mixed Marriage in Canada

According to the 2006 census, 3.9% of the 7,482,800 couples in Canada were mixed unions. Mixed unions between one visible minority group member and one nonmember or between persons belonging to two different visible groups accounted for 289,400 couples overall. In comparison, mixed unions represented 3.1% of all couples in 2001 and 2.6% in 1991. Between 2001 and 2006, mixed unions grew at a rapid pace (33%), more than five times the growth for all couples (6.0%). There are several reasons why the proportion of mixed unions may be increasing. For example, there could be more mixed unions as people meet, interact and form relationships in many different social, educational or work-related settings. The growth of mixed unions may also be due to an increasing number of people who belong to visible minority groups, resulting in greater potential for people to meet spouses or partners from outside their group.

Anne Milan, Hélène Maheux, and Tina Chui,
"A Portrait of Couples in Mixed Unions,"
Statistics Canada, April 4, 2010.

my mother began pressuring me to go with a nice Chinese boy. Alas, there weren't any in the vicinity, nice or otherwise.

My high school history courses didn't mention the 1923 Chinese Immigration Act, which slammed the door shut on Chinese (and led to my aforementioned prom problem). And my Canadian-born parents never spoke of the systemic discrimination they experienced, including the denial of voting rights until 1947. For years, I chafed at their apparent bigotry. Gradually, as I learned bits of my family history—that my grandfather arrived in 1881 to help build the Canadian Pacific Railway, and that my three other grandparents, who came slightly later, paid the head tax—I realized my parents were clinging to our Chinese heritage for fear of rejection or persecution by the mainstream.

A Scary Future

I believe this is what we are seeing in Toronto today. New arrivals come burdened with the past, fearing for the future, not yet understanding that it will be unimaginably different from everything they left behind. They cling to the hijab or the ceremonial dagger, sometimes beyond reason. On rare occasions strict adherence to Old World values has devastating consequences. (When 16-year-old Aqsa Parvez now famously tried to ditch the veil—and avoid an arranged marriage—her father and brother strangled her to death.) But overwhelmingly, in a generation or two, immigrants integrate.

The Role of Business

In the meantime, big corporations and leaders in the financial services industry are bending over backwards trying to tap into new Canadian markets. In the past couple of years, the Royal Bank [of Canada, or RBC] has recruited 100 immigrants from China, India, the Middle East and Latin America as personal account managers. The majority of the new hires had financial services experience, and many were prominent in their communities. "When we have a new immigrant client, we can make a perfect match," says Zabeen Hirji, RBC's human resources chief. "We're in the business of giving advice, and that requires trust."

RBC has also launched a reciprocal mentoring program called Diversity Dialogues that pairs senior managers with visible minority employees several ranks below. Although it sounds like a politically correct PR manoeuvre, the "dialogue" is crassly pragmatic: The higher-up tells the junior employee how to get ahead at the bank, and the junior tells the higher-up how to, say, reach Chinese or South Asian immigrants with money. "It's beyond Diversity 101," says Hirji. "That's the power of Toronto. The social imperative and the business imperative are two sides of the same coin."

"Utterly at Home"

Visible minorities already constitute 43 per cent of RBC's 13,000 Toronto-area employees. More significantly, they make up 38 per cent of management and 14 per cent of executives. Of the nine-member executive team that reports directly to the bank's CEO [chief executive officer], Gord Nixon, two are visible minorities, including Hirji, a Tanzanian-born Indian who came to Canada at 14 and is married to someone she describes as "a Polish-Irish-American Canadian."

Hirji says she feels utterly at home in Toronto. And so do I. I'm not thrilled when the other parents in my Lawrence Park neighbourhood mistake me for a nanny. (Then again, when I lived in Beijing and my boys were little, the Chinese nannies assumed the same.)

Anyway, nature has the last laugh. My two sons don't resemble me at all—or my husband. They don't even look like brothers. One looks faintly Asian, the other 100 per cent Caucasian. Often, when we go out for Chinese food, my older son and I get chopsticks, while my husband and younger son are given forks. Without me as a visual clue, people sometimes think our older son is Italian or Spanish. With me as a visual clue, people are flummoxed by the hues of our younger son. The other day, the waitress at Congee Queen, the best Chinese restaurant in Don Mills, assumed he was a visiting hockey player from Scandinavia, probably because I had once taken several teenaged Danish players there for platters of beef chow mein.

"He's your son?" she said. "I thought he was from Denmark."

Finding Humour

My kids consider all this ethnic confusion rather hilarious. At 17, my younger son and his schoolmates satirize racism and, like the comedian Russell Peters, flip prejudice on its ugly head. The jokes go something like this: Hide your dog. Daryl's coming for lunch. Laughs ensue, including from Daryl, an ethnic Chinese. As long as the zinger smacks a stereotype, it works for any ethnic group.

The kids have boundaries: They won't make fun of anyone's acne or parents, and they won't bully anyone. But after that, anything goes. I love these kids. And I love this city. With ever-increasing numbers of mixed couples, Toronto is bursting with hybrid vigour. For years, everyone thought Toronto was an aboriginal word for "meeting place." It's not. It means "where there are trees standing in the water." Who cares? It's still a meeting place to me.

Periodical and Internet Sources Bibliography

The following articles have been selected to supplement the diverse views presented in this chapter.

Phil Barnes	"Korean Traditions Challenged as Mixed Marriages Soar," UPI.com, March 28, 2012.
Catholic Review	"Intermarriage Found More Common for Reform Jews, Less So for Catholics," October 31, 2010.
Ashley Hayes	"Study: Interracial Marriage, Acceptance Growing," CNN.com, February 16, 2012.
Sharon Jayson	"Interracial Marriage: More Accepted, Still Growing," *USA Today*, November 7, 2011.
Belinda Luscombe	"Modern Family: More Likely to Be Multigenerational, Unmarried or Interracial," *Time*, April 30, 2012.
Jill Mahoney	"More Canadians in Mixed Unions, Statscan Says," *Globe and Mail*, April 20, 2010.
David Morse	"Interracial Marriage Is Widely Accepted, but Not for Ad Families," *Ad Age*, March 16, 2012.
Emil Ovbiagele	"Love May Be Colorblind, but Others Aren't," *The Next Great Generation*, July 8, 2010.
Susan Saulny	"Interracial Marriage Seen Gaining Wide Acceptance," *New York Times*, February 16, 2012.
Michael Shelton	"Color Blind Love," *Psychology Today*, October 11, 2010.
Rachel L. Swarns	"For Asian-American Couples, a Tie That Binds," *New York Times*, March 30, 2012.

CHAPTER 2

Factors That Influence the Prevalence of Mixed Marriage

Malaysian Mixed Marriages Are Common and Accepted in Multicultural Society

M. Rajah

M. Rajah is a reporter for the Malaysia Star. *In the following viewpoint, Rajah criticizes a controversial comment by a Malaysian politician, who blamed the divorce of a national celebrity, Maya Karin, on the cultural and religious differences found in mixed marriages. Rajah reminds the readers that Malaysia has always been a multicultural country and has a long history of different races, ethnicities, and religions living together in harmony. In addition, Rajah states that these wrongheaded and divisive comments sharply contradict the "Malaysia concept," which was implemented to celebrate Malaysia's national unity.*

As you read, consider the following questions:

1. What heritage does the author believe that Malaysians in the peninsula will find if they dig hard enough?

2. According to Maximus Ongkili, what two Malaysian states have the highest percentage of mixed marriages in the country?

3. In what two Malaysian states does the author believe that the "Malaysia concept" has long been a reality?

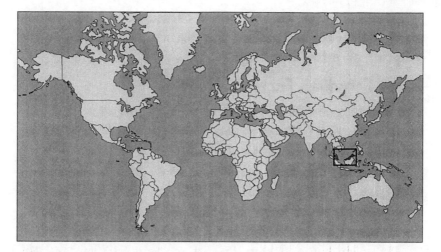

The issue of mixed marriages seems to be in the limelight these days, especially in peninsular Malaysia broadsheets and tabloids.

Why all the brouhaha about intermarriage? As far as Sabah and Sarawak [two Malaysian states] are concerned, it is a nonissue as such marriages are part and parcel of life.

A Controversial Comment

Recently, Information, Communication, and Culture Minister Datuk Seri Dr Rais Yatim made several dubious statements about mixed marriages when responding to questions from the media on celebrity Maya Karin's breakup with her *mat salleh* [a Westerner] husband.

He began with a statement directed at young couples to think long and hard before committing to a mixed marriage, citing findings by certain "scientific studies" that there was a higher rate of divorce among couples of mixed marriage.

The minister then went on to persecute mixed marriages between Muslims and non-Muslims and those with Westerners, blaming cultural and religious differences and the way a person is raised as key factors for the failure in mixed marriages.

Needless to say, his statements caused quite a stir among many Malaysians and ruffled the feathers of those in, or the offspring of, mixed marriages.

Same Forgotten Facts

The honourable minister seemed to have forgotten that Malaysia is a nation built on mixed marriages and Malaysians are generally already multicultural.

If they dig into their family tree roots deep enough, many Malaysians in the peninsula will find that they have heritage they probably never knew of—Siamese, Burmese, [Buginese], Portuguese, Chinese, Indian and a host of other ethnic groups.

Rais also seems to have forgotten about Sarawak and Sabah.

To say that the failure of marriage is caused by cultural differences or religions is inappropriate and shallow.

The factors contributing to the failure of a mixed marriage are no different from those in same-race-same-religion marriages.

Marriage Dynamics

Breakdown in marriages happens mainly because of lack of understanding between two people of different characters, lack of commitment, infidelity, dishonesty and neglect.

It would be wrong to say that mixed marriages had too many obstacles to overcome compared to same-race-same-religion marriages. There are no guarantees that same-race-same-religion marriages will be smooth sailing.

The success of a union between two individuals depends very much on their commitment, understanding and emotional strength to weather storms.

Any marriage, whether mixed or same race, is hard work.

Rais's statements also imply that those who enter into mixed marriages do not work at their marriages. Presumably, they do not "think a thousand times," as he put it, before taking the plunge.

Ethnic Demographics of Malaysia

Malaysia's multiracial society contains many ethnic groups. Malays and indigenous groups comprise 67.4% of the population. By constitutional definition, all Malays are Muslims. About a quarter of the population is ethnic Chinese, a group which historically has played an important role in trade and business. Malaysians of Indian descent comprise about 7% of the population and include Hindus, Muslims, Buddhists, and Christians.

Population density is highest in peninsular Malaysia, home to some 22.6 million of the country's 28.3 million inhabitants. The rest live on the Malaysian portion of the island of Borneo in the large but less densely populated states of Sabah and Sarawak. More than half of Sarawak's residents and about two-thirds of Sabah's are from indigenous groups.

"Background Notes: Malaysia," US State Department, March 2, 2012.

No person in his or her right mind will enter a marriage for the sake of getting a divorce.

It would be wrong to say that mixed marriages had too many obstacles to overcome compared to same-race-same-religion marriages.

Malaysia

His statements also sharply contradict Datuk Seri Najib Tun Razak's Malaysia concept[, which emphasizes ethnic harmony and national unity].

The prime minister, during his many recent visits to Sarawak, has commended and regarded the people of Sarawak as the most tolerant and united in the country.

He sang praises about how the people of Sarawak lived harmoniously despite the diversity in ethnicity and how mixed marriages here made unity more meaningful.

He has been promoting Sarawak as a model for the Malaysia concept.

Even before the Malaysia concept was introduced, Science, Technology and Innovation Minister Datuk Dr Maximus Ongkili, who was at one time in charge of national unity and integration, stated that Sarawak and Sabah had the highest percentage of mixed marriages and the unity, tolerance and bonds among the people in these states were pivotal ingredients in national integration.

One would not doubt the minister, who himself comes from the racially and culturally diverse land of Sabah.

A High Acceptance of Mixed Marriage

Sarawak's very own Chief Minister Tan Sri Abdul Taib Mahmud has talked about how hardly an eyebrow is raised in Sarawak when mixed marriages take place.

A Chinese marrying a Melanau, a *mat salleh* marrying an Orang Ulu, an Iban marrying an Indian, a Berawan marrying a Penan, a Malay marrying a Kelabit, a *mat salleh* marrying a Malay, a Lakiput marrying an Ukit, born Muslims marrying non-Muslims—these and many more interracial marriages are common in Sarawak.

Mixed marriages and racial integration can be likened to breathing in this Land of the Hornbill. It is a norm. It is practised almost unconsciously.

Sarawakians never needed to be told of the *muhibbah* or Malaysia concept. We never needed such concepts or slogans indoctrinated into us. Integration is everywhere in Sarawak.

Diversity in Malaysia

The degree of racial integration in Sarawak surpasses the expectations of many who come from culturally diverse countries such as the United States and Indonesia.

There are longhouses throughout Sarawak where one will find Chinese, Indians and Malays living with their indigenous spouses and their families.

There are also villages and longhouses where one would spot the occasional blue-eyed blond child whose *mat salleh* parent has settled down and dedicated his or her life to being with his or her spouse's community.

It has often been said (in good humour) that we Sarawakians apply for leave from work for almost every festive season because we have immediate family members who, through mixed marriages, celebrate Chinese New Year, Gawai [Dayak], Hari Raya, Deepavali and Christmas; and we have to go back to the longhouses or *kampungs* to be with our family members for the festivities.

While we take great pride in our respective ethnic groups and cultures, the people of Sarawak and Sabah do not refer to themselves as Malay, Chinese, Iban, Bidayuh, Dusun, Kadazan or any of the other ethnic groups. We are happy to refer to ourselves as Sarawakians or Sabahans.

[Intermarriage] has long been a reality in these two east Malaysian states.

Our counterparts and certain ministers and politicians from peninsular Malaysia have a lot to learn about tolerance, understanding and unity from us.

Japanese Women Are Influenced by the Media to Prefer Western Men

Rick Wallace

Rick Wallace is a reporter for the Australian. *In the following viewpoint, he examines the growing trend of Japanese women marrying Western men, a practice that has become more tolerated in Japanese society. Wallace reports that researchers blame the influence of media and advertising for this development. In many magazines and other media outlets, it has become fashionable to date or marry a Westerner. Researchers contend that these women are also motivated to escape cultural and gender roles in Japan.*

As you read, consider the following questions:

1. According to Wallace, by how much did the annual number of Japanese women marrying foreigners increase between 1980 and 2009?

2. According to the research of sociologist Beverley Yamamoto, what is the strange trend that emerged from her research on the rising numbers of Japanese women marrying Western men?

3. What does Wallace say is the attitude of Japanese men to the growing trend of Japanese women marrying Westerners?

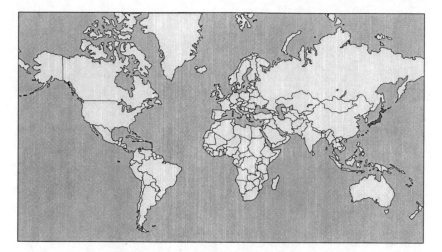

It was Japan's gay community—keen observers and labellers of social subclasses—that first came up with the word *gaisen*.

A slightly acerbic term used to describe Japanese women who prefer Western men, *gaisen*, or a subtler alternative, is likely to enter the broader vocabulary sometime soon, if it hasn't already.

Statistics show that more and more Japanese women are turning their backs on Japanese men and marrying Australian, American, European or British men. Mixed marriages in Japan, one of the most racially homogenous countries in the world, are on the rise.

The overall numbers are still small, but dating or marrying a Westerner has gained acceptance, if not a certain cachet or coolness in some social classes.

The Role of Media and Advertising

Osaka University sociologist Beverley Yamamoto, who studies this issue, says mass media and advertising are encouraging Japanese women to seek Western partners by presenting them as cool or desirable.

"If you look at a lot of the upmarket magazines aimed at women they usually show idealistic views of women, women out on their own," Yamamoto says.

"Where they show men, they are nearly always Western men—the two of them together pushing the buggy, or the two of them together taking the kids in the car ... so there's this idealised Western version of marriage, which I think is way more attractive to Japanese women."

Mixed marriages in Japan, one of the most racially homogenous countries in the world, are on the rise.

She says the view espoused by the magazines seemed to have taken root, relating the story of one of her graduate students who married a tall, good-looking Portuguese man. When they arrived at the reception, her friends were screaming at him as if he were a pop star.

"It kind of looks cool and sophisticated to be with this tall Western guy," she says.

"Whatever the difficulties of a cross-border marriage, and there are tons of them, that seemed to be their ideal."

A Rising Trend

The annual number of Japanese women recorded as marrying foreigners has increased by 165 per cent between 1980 and 2009. Since 2003, in most years the total has topped 8000.

Yamamoto says it tends to be well-educated and well-travelled Japanese women who seek Western men.

"My own research shows that women who marry Western men nearly always have had quite substantial periods of time overseas themselves, so they are quite mobile, so they have the skills and competence that go with that mobility," she says.

Reasons for This New Trend

Their motivation, she says, is an escape from the fairly rigid gender rules of a Japanese marriage that establish the husband

---

Japanese Men and Mixed Marriage

In Japan, of the 49,000 international marriages in 2006, some 40,000 of them involved a foreign bride and a Japanese man. . . .

The vast majority of the 40,000 marriages involving a Japanese male and non-Japanese (NJ) female were mail-order brides from the Philippines and China (24,000).

Imogen Reed,
"Mixed Marriages, Divorces and Kidnapping,"
Japan—It's a Wonderful Rife *(blog), May 29, 2012.*

---

as a breadwinner, leaving the wife in sole charge of most domestic or child-rearing duties.

"I think it's the idea that through that marriage they will have a freer relationship, a more liberal, gender-equal relationship," she says.

"They are often looking for a man that will be more helpful in terms of taking a bigger role in the home, be more demonstrative, be more emotional, talk about things more.

"They don't want the traditional middle-class Japanese man who maybe won't communicate that much, or will expect them to do all sorts of things in the home, or may not expect them to work. I think they have a dream, they want something more liberal in terms of gender relations."

An Interesting Aspect

But so far in her research a strange trend has emerged: As much as these women value the prospect of escaping gender roles in the arms of a Western man, those mixed couples usually conform to the Japanese way as long as they stay in Japan.

81

"My own research says, in reality, once they get married these Japanese women are fairly conservative in the way they structure their marriages.

"They often do take charge of the home and the domestic side.

"The couples I have looked at have all stayed in Japan and the culture here dominates more than the couples expect because there are family relations and family expectations and they are living in this society."

One of her graduate students, however, studied mixed Australian Japanese couples who moved to Australia and found they took on a more Western way of life, with both of them working, sharing home duties and socialising together more.

Advantages of Mixed Marriage for Japanese Women

Ayano Pankhurst, a young Japanese woman married to translator Alex Pankhurst, an Australian, fits the description offered by Yamamoto.

She studied in Australia as an exchange student and while she says she never hunted for a foreigner, she always thought an international marriage might be a possibility.

"My experience with my husband is that there is a difference between Western and Japanese men in how they express their affection and care to their partners and families," Ayano says.

"The way they value others is just different. I think Japanese girls tend to feel they can live happily ever after with Western men, even in old age.

"We tend to have an image for the Japanese couples that they do not get along with each other any longer as they get old, but at least from my experience I can be confident that we can stay in love with each other and get along with each other still then."

Alex is also happy and struggles to find a disadvantage to international marriage.

"It offers a perspective on Japanese culture that most people who just come here to work or study just don't get. It gives me a much closer look at family life here in Japan," he says.

Challenges

The one challenge, he says, will be deciding where they want to live and bring up their daughter, Emma, who's almost two.

"We can't really decide which way we want to go at the moment—it's almost like we are staying in Japan out of inertia rather than making an actual decision to stay here," he says. "We have very understanding families, so it hasn't been too bad. I know some people have parents who are opposed to the marriage."

Where couples do report tensions, Yamamoto has found they tend to be complaints from the men, who might be resenting the fact their wife is unwilling or unable to work amid worsening economic circumstances, or that the wife is following traditional Japanese patterns of socialising with female friends rather than as a couple.

Consequences of This Trend

So with this trend favouring Western men, do Japanese men feel maligned?

And how do they feel about losing a cohort of otherwise eligible women to foreigners?

There are Internet forums in Japan that deal with such lifestyle choices and those who profess a taste for Western men can usually expect a rough time at [the] hands of those with nationalistic tendencies, which are not far beneath the surface in some inhabitants of a country that's historically been proud of its racial purity.

But this is far from the mainstream view among Japanese men, who are perhaps more bemused than angry about this trend.

Kazu, a single Japanese in his mid-30s, says over a few drinks at a Tokyo izakaya (or pub) that he struggles to understand the motivation of women who prefer Western men.

He doesn't necessarily resent the fact such tastes make a significant number of otherwise available Japanese women off-limits, but he does wonder what the appeal is.

The Lure of the Exotic

Kazu puts it down to foreign guys having a sense of mystique about them, particularly for those Japanese women who aren't particularly worldly.

He agrees that a taste for the exotic is human nature in a sense, a hardwired genetic protection against breeding only with your own (although it must be said that, if so, it's only recently caught on in Japan).

There are Internet forums in Japan that deal with such lifestyle choices and those who profess a taste for Western men can usually expect a rough time at [the] hands of those with nationalistic tendencies, which are not far beneath the surface in some inhabitants of a country that's historically been proud of its racial purity.

Kazu rejects the suggestion that these women are simply being pragmatic and opting out of the demands put on them by Japanese men, who have a reputation for working punishing hours, leaving their wives to a lonely life of home drudgery.

This, he says, is a stereotype that should have died with his parents' generation. Younger Japanese men are just as open to sharing housework, parental duties and career advancement as Western men.

Northern Ireland's Acceptance of Catholic-Protestant Marriages Is Based on Class and Economic Factors

Katrina Lloyd and Gillian Robinson

Katrina Lloyd is research director and Gillian Robinson is direc-tor of ARK, a resource for social and political information on Northern Ireland. In the following viewpoint, the authors find that there is a dearth of information on Catholic-Protestant couples in Northern Ireland, with what research there is based on very small samples of mixed-religion marriages and partner-ships. Lloyd and Robinson report that the research shows that people in mixed-religion relationships are younger, better edu-cated, and have significantly higher incomes than those couples in same-religion partnerships. The authors recommend that more in-depth research be done on the characteristics of mixed-religion couples in Northern Ireland before a comprehensive analysis of the trend can be completed.

As you read, consider the following questions:

1. According to the 2001 census, what percentage of people in Northern Ireland are involved in mixed-religion marriages or relationships?

Katrina Lloyd and Gillian Robinson, "Intimate Mixing—Bridging the Gap? Catholic-Protestant Relationships in Northern Ireland," ARK, April 2008. Copyright © 2008 by ARK Queen's University Belfast/University of Ulster. All rights reserved. Reproduced by permission.

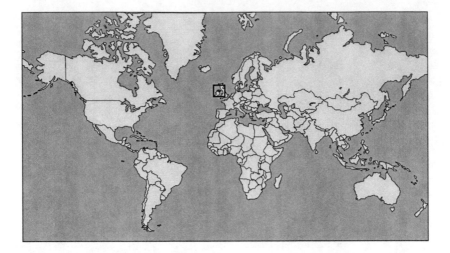

2. What percentage of the people in Northern Ireland involved in mixed-religion marriages or partnerships were under the age of forty-five years, according to census figures?

3. What percentage of mixed-religion couples in Northern Ireland were employed, according to census figures?

It is well documented in the research literature that Northern Ireland is a divided society where members of the two main religious groups, Catholics and Protestants, have limited opportunities to meet and interact with each other due to segregation in a number of key areas of social life. The main focus of interest in segregation in Northern Ireland has been on education and housing, and attempts have been made throughout the years of what are often termed the 'Troubles' to encourage religious mixing through integrated schools and mixed-religion housing estates. Such efforts are based on the theory that bringing people together to interact in social situations can improve intergroup relations and remove prejudices—reported in the research literature as the 'contact hypothesis'. Indeed, successive governments have implemented a number of initiatives and spent millions of pounds to encourage contact between Catholics and Protestants and improve community relations in Northern Ireland.

Mixed Marriages in Northern Ireland

One area of contact that has received little attention is that of intimate mixing between Catholics and Protestants through marriage or co-habitation. According to the Northern Ireland Mixed Marriage Association (NIMMA) mixed marriages, by the fact that they happen at all, can be seen as a start of the reconciliation which is so crucial for peace in Northern Ireland. NIMMA suggests that when communities intermarry families become inextricably linked and may gradually come to lose the fear they may have of one another. Such outcomes can contribute to the promotion of good relations and the development of a shared future, as advocated by the government in Northern Ireland.

Although there are no official statistics on the number of mixed religion marriages or partnerships in Northern Ireland, figures from the latest census (2001) and from social attitudes surveys estimate that it is somewhere between 5% and 12%. There is also a dearth of information on the characteristics and attitudes of the people who choose to enter into such relationships. What research evidence there is on mixed-religion partnerships in Northern Ireland has generally been based on small samples of married couples using qualitative data collection methods that are difficult to generalise to the population as a whole. This is partly due to the small number of respondents living in mixed-religion relationships picked up in surveys of random samples of the population in any one year. Each year around 10% of respondents to the NILT [Northern Ireland Life and Times] Survey say their partner is a different religion to them. As this is a small number, it is not possible to carry out detailed analyses on the characteristics and attitudes of those who choose to marry or live with people who are of a different religion to them. To overcome this problem, a data set has been created that pools eight years (1998 to 2005) of information on respondents to the NILT Survey and which contains questions that have been asked in all eight years. Using this method, the number of respondents who say their partner is a different religion than they are is 802. This represents 10% of all respondents who had partners (8,299).

This research update uses the pooled data set to examine the characteristics and attitudes of people who have chosen to enter into mixed-religion relationships to establish baseline figures for comparison in future years as Northern Ireland emerges from conflict into a new era of peace in which such relationships may become an accepted and normal part of society.

According to the Northern Ireland Mixed Marriage Association (NIMMA) mixed marriages, by the fact that they happen at all, can be seen as a start of the reconciliation which is so crucial for peace in Northern Ireland.

Marital Status and Age

[Three] times as many respondents who were in mixed-religion partnerships were not married as those who lived with a partner who was the same religion as they were (12% and 4% respectively). They also tended to be younger than their same-religion counterparts with 56% being under the age of 45 years compared with 39%. Anecdotal evidence suggests that some people in mixed relationships may choose not to marry because of the complexities involved in deciding where to marry and so on.

Socio-Economic Status

There is a suggestion that mixed marriage is predominantly a middle-class phenomenon. Evidence from the NILT Survey partly supports this contention. Respondents in mixed-religion

Marital Status and Age Group by Type of Relationship in Northern Ireland

Marital Status*	Same Religion %	Mixed Religion %
Married	96	88
Living as married	4	12
Total	100	100
Age Group*		
18–24 years	2	4
25–34 years	13	22
35–44 years	24	30
45–54 years	24	26
55–64 years	21	13
65+ years	17	6
Total	100	100

*statistically significant p<0.001

TAKEN FROM: Northern Ireland Life and Times, 2005.

partnerships had significantly higher incomes and better educational qualifications than those of their counterparts living in same-religion partnerships. At the lowest end of the income scale 48% of respondents who were living in same-religion partnerships had an income which was less than £10,000 per annum compared with 37% of those who were living in mixed-religion partnerships. Conversely, more of the latter than the former had annual incomes of £30,000 or more (11% and 7% respectively). Two in five (41%) respondents living with someone who was a different religion than they were had qualifications that were of A-level standard or above compared with only 27% of respondents who lived with someone of the same religion. [Researchers] suggest that higher educational levels are generally associated with 'less virulent out-group attitudes' and research studies carried out in Northern Ireland have shown that contact at the university level has a positive effect on attitudes towards the 'other' group. [There] were no significant differences in relation to the respondents' social class (based on current or previous job).

Reflecting the age difference noted above, many more respondents who were living in mixed-religion partnerships were employed (64%) and fewer were retired (10%) than those who were living with people who had the same religion as them (53% and 21% respectively).

Other Factors Related to Living in Mixed-Religion Partnerships

[Respondents] who lived in mixed-religion partnerships (35%) were significantly more likely [than] those who did not (21%) to have lived outside Northern Ireland for more than six months. They were also more likely than their same-religion counterparts to say they had attended either formally integrated or mixed schools—16% of respondents who lived in mixed-religion partnerships said they had attended an integrated or mixed school compared with 11% of those whose partner was the same religion as them. In addition, nearly twice as many respondents (32%) who were in a mixed-religion partnership as those who were not (17%) said that a child in their care had attended a mixed-religion school in Northern Ireland.

There is a suggestion that mixed marriage is a predominantly middle-class phenomenon.

Party Support and Identity

[Researchers] reported that people who had attended formally integrated or mixed-religion schools in Northern Ireland appeared to have less sectarian views than those who attended schools with pupils only of the same religion as themselves. They were also 'more likely to reject traditional identities and allegiances than those who had attended a segregated one'. In line with these findings, [statistics show] that significantly more adults who were in mixed-religion relationships (17%) than those who were not (6%) said they supported the Alliance Party. They were also much more likely than respondents in same-religion partnerships to say they were neither Nationalist nor Unionist (59% and 27% respectively).

What the Research Shows

The findings show that there are differences in the socio-demographic characteristics of people who live in mixed-religion partnerships compared with their contemporaries who live in same-religion partnerships. The former tend to be younger, better educated and to have higher incomes, although they do not differ in their social class, at least as defined by their current or most recent job. These findings support previous results based on small-scale qualitative research carried out with mixed-religion married couples which suggested that mixed marriage is predominantly a middle-class phenomenon. In addition to differences in socio-economic characteristics, this research also found that there was significant variation in two important areas of contact with the 'other' community between those who were in mixed-religion partnerships and those who were not; namely the former were more likely to have spent time outside Northern Ireland and to have attended mixed-religion schools. Many more of them also said that a child in their care had attended a mixed-religion school. Furthermore, respondents who were in mixed-religion partnerships tended to reject traditional identities and allegiances compared to those who were in same-religion partnerships. This was shown by the fact that respondents in mixed-religion partnerships were less likely to align themselves with what are traditionally perceived to be Catholic (e.g., Sinn Féin) and Protestant (e.g., DUP [Democratic Unionist Party]) political parties and more likely to reject Unionist and Nationalist identities than those in same-religion relationships. These findings add to the weight of evidence suggesting that contact with the 'other' community may have long-term benefits in promoting a less sectarian outlook which may help to bridge the gap between Catholics and Protestants that exists in Northern Ireland.

Overall, this research has provided much-needed information on the characteristics and attitudes of people in Northern Ireland who live in mixed-religion partnerships. The analysis was, of course, restricted by the number and scope of time-series questions that are asked in the NILT Survey each year. It is recommended that more research is carried out into mixed-religion partnerships in Northern Ireland. This research could be expanded to include groups that people outside Northern Ireland might consider mixed, such as Christian/non-Christian and mixed ethnic backgrounds.

Indonesia Has Made Legal Improvements for Mixed Marriages

Nani Afrida

Nani Afrida is a reporter for the Jakarta Post. *In the following viewpoint, she recommends that Indonesian women planning on marrying foreign men do copious research on their rights under the law, looking specifically to the example of other couples that have had experience maneuvering around Indonesia's discriminatory laws. Afrida contends that many couples blame the Indonesian government for the lack of information for couples that forces them to utilize the Internet and other resources. Recent improvements to Indonesian citizenship and immigration laws better address the legal issues surrounding mixed marriage, but the government has failed to publicize the changes and provide better access to information.*

As you read, consider the following questions:

1. How many members does Afrida report are there in the Indonesian Mixed Marriage Society (PerCa)?

2. How long does a required temporary stay permit (KITAS) allow a foreigner to stay in Indonesia?

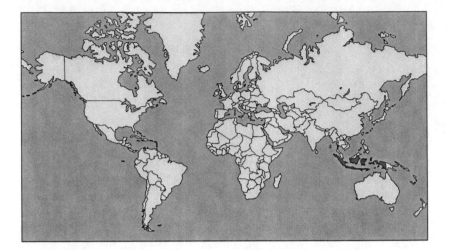

3. According to the author, how many foreigners applied for KITAS due to marriage in 2011?

A foreign husband is a challenge for an Indonesian woman. She must be ready to have her rights as an Indonesian downgraded, as well as to be extorted by officials. However, the many bad experiences of previous mixed couples have become good lessons for new couples.

Doing Her Research

Renny Mayasari, 36, is one Indonesian who had prepared everything before marrying her Dutch husband.

"I did some research about marrying foreigners on the Internet and I found a lot of information from friends who had already gone through the process," she said.

Unlike some other Indonesian women who were barred from owning property due to their foreign marriages, Renny was fully aware that she needed a prenuptial agreement to allow her to purchase a house and other things.

"I still dream of developing my tourism business in Indonesia. This prenuptial agreement will allow me to have property, even though my husband is a foreigner," Renny said, laughing.

Tini, 29, the wife of an Australian, also found important information about marrying foreigners on the Internet, including blogs written by mixed-marriage couples.

"When I processed my papers to the local religious affairs office [KUA], the officer asked for some money to expedite the process. When I asked him which regulation provided for that, he stopped pushing me," Tini said.

She said that she did the paperwork herself at a lower cost than if the couple had hired an agency.

The Role of the Internet

Before the Internet, mixed couples were often trapped in troublesome situations, which some blamed on lack of information from the government on the rights and consequences of Indonesians marrying foreigners.

"No one tells you about the importance of prenuptial agreements. Probably because this is not their business," said Pijay, 30, an Indian citizen.

Today Indonesia has two laws—the citizenship law and the immigration law—that address mixed marriages. However, some of the laws overlap with previously existing legislation on marriage and labor.

"This is why I don't have a house or land even though I am married to an Indonesian. We were married in a hurry, and we knew nothing about prenuptial agreements," he said.

However, mixed couples have found that one can put their children's names on documents when buying property, or in the case of minors, they can appoint other family members as the children's guardians.

Protecting the Rights of Women and Children

Many Indonesian women married to foreigners such as Renny and Tini know that they are protected by the law—at least on paper.

Today Indonesia has two laws—the citizenship law and the immigration law—that address mixed marriages. However, some of the laws overlap with previously existing legislation on marriage and labor.

The Indonesian Mixed Marriage Society (PerCa), which has around 250 members, mostly in Batam, Jakarta and Denpasar, welcomed the new laws, which allowed for dual citizenship for children before they came of age.

However some of the society's members said many children of mixed marriages lost their Indonesian citizenship due to their parents' ignorance of the law.

The 2006 Citizenship Law

Article 41 of the citizenship law stipulated that children born to mixed-marriage couples before the law was enacted had until Aug. 1, 2010, to obtain Indonesian citizenship.

After that date, children born before Aug. 1, 2006, would automatically be registered as foreign citizens, as was the case before the law was passed.

Rulita Anggraini, the chairwoman of PerCa, said the government failed to promote the 2006 citizenship law, particularly in border regions, where many Indonesians were married to foreigners.

"We are still striving to ask for more time from the government" regarding the arrangement of children's citizenship, she said.

Previously, many Indonesian women could not retain custody of their children after their foreign husbands completed their jobs in Indonesia. The children usually followed their fathers back to their countries. To stay with their mothers required temporary stay permits (KITAS) or permanent stay permits (KITAP).

A KITAS allows foreigners to stay up to 24 months in Indonesia, while a KITAP allows foreigners to stay in Indonesia up to five years.

The Downside

Although the costs are about Rp [rupiah] 3 million to extend a temporary-stay permit, the process is a notorious red tape headache. Many foreigners prefer to hire agencies, even though it makes the costs much higher.

Eva is one of the lucky women who benefited from the 2006 citizenship law. Her husband, a citizen of Senegal, died in 2006, leaving her with a baby boy.

"I was so lucky, because the law allowed me to register my boy as an Indonesian citizen, so I don't need to pay for a KITAS or KITAP. I cannot imagine the future of my son with a foreign nationality, when he knows no one in Senegal," Eva said.

The citizenship law also allows children to possess dual nationalities until they are 21 years old. In case the children decide to follow their foreign parent, they can more easily obtain a permanent-stay permit.

The Revised Immigration Law

The new immigration law allows for permits for foreigners married to Indonesians.

"The new revision of the immigration law is based on humanity. We know that it will be difficult for foreigners to visit their families in Indonesia, so we adjusted the regulation," Maryoto [Sumadi], the spokesman of the Immigration Directorate General said.

Since the amended immigration law was passed last year [2011], the number of foreigners applying for visas sponsored by their spouses increased.

The number of foreigners asking for KITAS due to marriage jumped from 166 foreigners in 2010 to 3,794 in 2011, 2,365 of whom were men.

"Now, it is easier to be married to foreigners," Tini said. "As long as you have all the information."

Interfaith Marriages in the Philippines Are Based on Common Heritage

Tingting Cojuangco

Tingting Cojuangco is a columnist for the Philippine Star *and the president of the Philippine Public Safety College. In the following viewpoint, she maintains that mixed marriages between Christians and Muslims have a long history in the Philippines. Although the religions have different teachings and customs, their differences are overshadowed by common values and traditions that were in place long before Muslim and Christian missionaries came to the Philippines to convert citizens. Cojuangco argues that the two religions "run parallel and have mutually enriched each other over the centuries" and facilitate a proud tradition of mixed-religion marriages in the country.*

As you read, consider the following questions:

1. According to the author, when did the people of Sulu learn about Islam?

2. How many wives does the author say a Muslim husband is allowed?

3. According to legend, what does ascendancy from the Noni lineage mean?

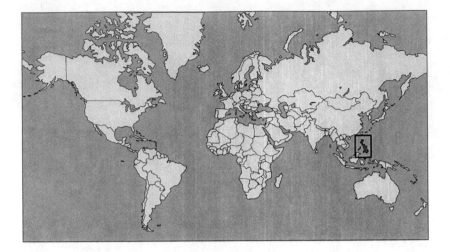

Holy Week and days of relaxation and religiosity bring to mind Muslim and Christian marriages. It all began with the marriage of Sharif Kabungsuan from Malacca in 1515 to Putri Tunina, daughter of the Manobo chieftain. He married a second time to another Manobo, Surabanon.

The Legends

Legends say that Muslims who sailed in a *caldron* for the Philippines were either royalty, merchants or missionaries of Arab descent from South China, Indonesia, Borneo and the Malay peninsula. They docked in Sulu, Central Mindanao, Palawan, southern Luzon and the Visayas. The titles of these early missioners were *auliya, makhdumin, sayid*, and *shariff*, indicating that they were well versed in the doctrines and laws of Islam. From them, the people of Sulu [an island province] in 1380 and Mindanao [an island province] in 1515 learned about Muhammad as the Prophet of Allah.

Spreading Christianity, on the other hand, was not necessarily a tool for colonialism. The Treaty of Tordesillas encouraged seafarers and discoverers to venture to faraway lands after Christopher Columbus returned from the New World. The world was then divided between Spain and Portugal: East of

Cape Verde belonged to Portugal and west to Spain. The Christian missionaries were Augustinians, Franciscans, Dominicans, Jesuits and Recollects—they all came accompanying these adventurers in search of lands to conquer, to escape oppression or participate in abundant sea trading. From them we learned of our Holy Bible.

In both Christianity and Islam, there were certain traditions and customs that obviously could be tolerated, while others were incompatible and unacceptable to both. But, on this side of the world, no matter what indoctrination or approach was introduced with a new set of beliefs, there were certain native values that could not be uprooted. They were planted long before the introduction of these two religions.

Cultural Difference Between Muslims and Christians

The Muslim husband is allowed four wives. Kabungsuan married three times. Being allowed to marry four times has always fascinated Christians because few know that the first wife and her children are able to accept the second wife, the succeeding ones and their children.

The first wife can be very assertive before and after her husband takes in another wife. And why not? Her permission is needed for the husband to do so. In the household hierarchy, the first wife takes the prime status with the second and succeeding wives taking on subordinate roles. The management of the household rests on her, with major housekeeping activities remaining within the sphere of her influence.

This is not to say that Moro [a population of indigenous Muslims in the Philippines] women are not held in high esteem. They always have been respected—just read the 980 A.D. epic *Darangen*.

"The *Inoyanan* or Sultan called all the datus to an assembly. Anyone could present a problem, which was discussed in order to arrive at a common answer. This answer was presented to the *pameli'iyan* who approved or returned it for further discussion. After a decision was taken, it was presented to the *panabiya'an* who likewise approved or returned it for more discussion. If approved, it was presented to the *kasango'an a Adil* who approved or disapproved it. If disapproved, the question was now thrown to the ladies, whose decision the assembly had binded itself to accept."

The women had the final say in all those meetings!

Christians, especially women, wonder if the Muslim wife does not feel insecure, throws tantrums and delivers threats. They do, since their husbands may at any time take in someone else to share her bed and responsibilities, rights and privileges.

In both Christianity and Islam, there were certain traditions and customs that obviously could be tolerated, while others were incompatible and unacceptable to both. But, on this side of the world, no matter what indoctrination or approach was introduced with a new set of beliefs, there were certain native values that could not be uprooted.

The Decline of Polygamy in the Philippines

My observation is that in the 21st century, Moro men generally do not marry four times anymore. Braver and bolder women know about women's rights and liberation. Schooling has introduced modern values. Some women won't nurture supportive roles to their husbands and his other wives. Communication facilities, especially cell phones, have allowed the fast movement of information with pictures, an addition to a woman's spies or friends that hinder married men from pursuing another woman. Then there is the high cost of living, which discourages men from maintaining a very large family.

Islam and the Philippines

Islam touched the shores of the Philippine islands way before American and Spanish colonizers did. The Islamization of the Philippine archipelago was part of the spread of the religion in the Southeast Asian region. Islam is not merely a religion, as noted by many Muslim scholars but is as well a way of life. Thus, when Islam spread throughout the country, it also introduced a system of government and a sophisticated culture.

Islam introduced a highly developed political structure, the sultanate. The traditional Muslim social structure in the Philippines was headed by a sultan who assumed both religious and secular authority. The Datu assumed communal leadership, providing aid and arbitration through agama courts under his leadership. The wealth amassed by the conquests of the Datu is provided to his subjects for aid, employment, and protection when needed. Interestingly, the Datu is not determined by their wealth but by the number of his followers. Further, the holy Qur'an, the source of both secular and religious percepts and laws of Muslims, provides a sense of oneness and fraternal bond between Muslims as an Ummah or Islamic Nation. Islam changed the country's once fragmented nature into a single nation.

"Institutional Strengthening of the Shari'a Justice System (Phase 1),
Final Report," United Nations Development Programme
and Supreme Court of the Philippines, June 2004.

The Challenge of Interfaith Marriage

Muslim men face the responsibility of convincing their future Christian wives to convert to Islam and have their children raised in the Islamic faith. Young Muslim women are less likely to marry non-Muslim men. They may actually feel infatuation for Christian men, but they tend to subvert those feelings. Muslim boys are given the opportunity to explain to their parents their desire to live out their dreams, while few women can.

Parents are likely to insist on their children's adherence to pure marriages. Don't we Christians do the same, whether for religion or race? As parents, we insist our decisions take precedence, whether it's about our children's relationships or schooling. But as Nellie [a character] or Mitzi Gaynor [the actress playing Nellie] sings in *South Pacific*, "We've got to be taught from year to year to hate all the people your family hates, you get to be carefully taught. . . . It goes on to the color of the skin where many judgments begin."

Now, a very unique situation are the Royal Nonis [an indigenous group] of Lanao del Sur [a province of the Philippines]. Vice-Mayor Sultan Quirino Sampiano, of Balabagan, explained the Noni lineage to me. It is a revered union that began in Lanao del Sur with the marriage of the Iranun Royal Amatunding of Butig municipality, to the sister of Sultan Kudarat of Maguindanao, whose name was Gayang. It was an accidental marriage, this royal marriage between a half-brother and half-sister. The consequence? Purity of blood.

The Royal Noni Legend

The story goes like this:

Sharif Kabungsuan, a prince from Johore, alighted in Tubok (now Malabang) and married the daughter of Datu Gandar of Malabang. Their marriage was blessed with a son named Saripada Maka'alang.

Maka'alang married a Bilaan woman and begot Bankaya. Bankaya married three women. First was his aunt Maganot. Maganot and Bankaya begot the father of Kudarat. The other wife of Bankaya begot Dimasangkay and the third wife begot Gugu Sarikula.

Dimasangkay married two women, one from Simuay, Maguindanao, and the other from Butig, Lanao del Sur. From his Butig wife he begot a girl, Omon, and from his Simuay wife he begot a boy, M'Borong.

The separated half-siblings Omon and M'Borong lost track of each other. Then they met and married each other without knowing they were half-brother and half-sister. Their offspring were known as the Noni, signifying purity of blood because of the intermarriages of both royalty. Omon and M'Borong begot a son, Amatunding, whose great-grandparents were of royal blood from Kabungsuan, and his women, the royal wife Angintabu. Amatunding married his first cousin Gayang, sister of Qudarat and daughter of Buisan. The offspring of Amatunding and Gayang marked the beginning of the Maranao ancestry. Interesting how Maranao intermarriages produced royalty!

Commonalities do bind us all.

Ascendancy from the Noni lineage is a political advantage. One who does not belong to a Noni family may surely lose in a political exercise. If two Nonis compete, their financial and political status will foretell their victory. Their educational background is regarded as less important than their family lineage.

A Common Culture

We cannot overlook that respect for parents is a value that has been ingrained in the very core of our society. This is a given for both Muslim and Christian families.

Commonalities do bind us all. We're all brothers, Muslim and Christian Filipinos, heirs to the 7,107 islands of the Philippines. Two currents in our Filipino culture run parallel and have mutually enriched each other over the centuries.

One religion came from Arabia, the other from Spain, but our blood and our skin, our minds and our hearts, whatever faith we profess, were born in our land.

Periodical and Internet Sources Bibliography

The following articles have been selected to supplement the diverse views presented in this chapter.

Veeramalla Anjaiah	"The Herculean Task of Becoming an Indonesian Family," *Jakarta Post*, May 15, 2012.
Sarah Britten	"Does That Poster Get Under Your Skin?," *Thought Leader* (blog), January 24, 2012.
Melissa Burkley	"Pop and Prejudice: How Modern Prejudice Is Depicted in Our Pop Culture," *Psychology Today*, September 25, 2009.
Emma Daly	"Sarajevo's Lingering Tensions," *International Herald Tribune*, April 8, 2012.
Eric Deggans	"On TV, Interracial Couples in a Too-Perfect World," NPR.org, March 4, 2011.
Alexia Elejalde-Ruiz	"Interracial Marriage: Mixing in Matching," *Chicago Tribune*, July 11, 2012.
IRIN	"Lebanon: Hotchpotch of Religious Laws Restricts Basic Rights," July 19, 2011.
Kevin Noble Maillard	"Playing the Interracial Card," *New York Times*, July 12, 2012.
M.S.	"Miscegenation and the South," *Economist*, March 13, 2012.
Kate Sheppard	"'The Loving Story': How an Interracial Couple Changed a Nation," *Mother Jones*, February 13, 2012.
Michele Somerville	"Chelsea and Marc: Their Mixed Marriage, a Mixed Blessing," *Huffington Post*, August 2, 2010.

GLOBAL VIEWPOINTS

CHAPTER 3

Barriers to Mixed Marriage

India Is Not Fully Accepting of Interfaith Marriages

Vimla Patil

Vimla Patil is an Indian journalist, columnist, and writer. In the following viewpoint, she identifies interreligious marriage as a controversial issue in Indian society. Patil notes that although there have been a number of high-profile celebrity mixed marriages in India, many people do not accept or support such unions. One reason is that many Indian families, especially parents, want to avoid the potential problems that may come with dealing with religious and cultural differences. According to Patil, it is very important for couples to support each other and garner the support of parents and other family members.

As you read, consider the following questions:

1. According to Patil, who do Indian parents look to as support in their old age?
2. What Indian celebrity couple does the author say recently got married and became a high-profile mixed-religion marriage?
3. According to Srilata Ghosh, what percentage of Indians are profoundly religious?

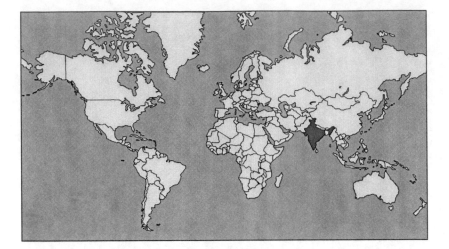

"This is 2012 yaar! We are in the 21st century! Why are we even talking about inter-religious marriages? They have the same chance of success as any other.

"Any two people can make a success of their relationship if they work well together," says Anu Desai-Khan, a young, successful investment banker—a Gujarati Hindu married to a Kerala Muslim for five years. "The days of fighting over religious beliefs are gone and young Indians should accept that as diverse communities come together for education, employment, travel and social networking, there are bound to be more inter-religious marriages. I met my husband at work and we decided to have a civil marriage to avoid religious problems in the two families. However, both our families are unhappy about our marriage and we have opted not to connect with them anymore."

A Tricky Question

Anu has brought up a very significant point that bothers present-day Indian society. Taking this point forward, actor Pooja Bedi says, "Why is it that people date people from other religious communities and then back out at the time of marriage saying there is opposition from the family? No matter how open-minded couples in love may be, they should discuss religious differences before they tie the knot. Relationships that lead to marriage are serious and haste can lead to disaster." Pooja Bedi herself was married to a Muslim and is now divorced and has two children.

Though Bollywood has any number of examples of 'happily married' inter-religion couples, Indian society as a whole, according to social observers, has yet to truly accept interreligious marriages. "The more liberal or non-religious the couple, the better are the chances of success for them," says Manda Pachauri, a counselor. "But some couples do lose their families in the acrimony and defiance which surrounds the marriage!"

Scrutinizing Bollywood

Pachauri's words are proved by an audit of Bollywood. Here, one can list numerous A-list Hindu-Muslim or Muslim-Christian marriages that have failed or succeeded because of reasons other than religion. Aamir Khan was married to Reena Dutta and had two children, Junaid and Ira, both brought up as Muslims. After his divorce, he married Kiran Rao and has a son called Azad Rao Khan.

Shah Rukh Khan is married to a Hindu (Gauri) and has two children—Aryan and Suhana—whose upbringing is secular from all reports. Salman Khan is the son of a Muslim father (Salim) and a Hindu mother (Sushila). He and his siblings Arbaaz, Suhail and Alvira have been brought up as secular Muslims. Arbaaz is married to Malaika Arora who is a Catholic and Sohail is married to Seema Sachdev, a Hindu. The family celebrates Id [Eid al-Fitr], Christmas and Ganesh Chaturthi with equal enthusiasm.

However, when Zayed Khan married Malaika Parekh, she converted to Islam and had a nikah [Muslim marriage]. His cousin Fardeen Khan married Natasha, the daughter of actors

Intercaste Marriages in India

In contemporary India, interracial marriages are more likely to involve spouses from the same social class. Previous studies are evident that marriage in India is still predominantly endogamous than exogamous: within same caste, same religion, and same economic group. One of the critical aspects of mixed marriages in Indian context is intercaste marriages. The concept of caste system discrimination is like a bane on the path of India's progress. In India, lower castes are not only deprived socially but also economically. For centuries, Indian society has been divided on the basis of caste system. The problem of caste system was so deep-rooted that it took years for the Indians to come out of that idea. Even today India is struggling to come out of this social menace. History reveals that efforts have been made by various social reformers and individuals whose names don't appear in the pages of history to make India free from the clutches of caste system, untouchability and race discrimination. And when we talk about Indian marriages, which are intercaste and interreligious, it seems like a taboo to most of the people.

Deepti Singh and Srinivas Goli,
"Exploring the Concept of Mixed Marriages
in Indian and Selected States: First Time Evidences from
Large Scale Survey," Population Association of America, 2011.

Mumtaz and Mayur Madhvani. Sanjay Dutt, himself the son of the inter-religion marriage of Nargis and Sunil Dutt, was married to a Hindu (Richa Sharma with whom he has a daughter) and is now married to Manyata aka Dilnawaz Shaikh through a Hindu ceremony. However, their twins have Islamic names: Shahraan and Iqra.

Other Factors

The above facts may prove that inter-religious marriages are successful when both partners and their families provide security, love and support to each other. Religion is not the biggest issue in their relationships. Having a lot of money, success and more than adequate personal space also helps. But among the *aam janata* [general public], this is often not so. Parents who often have just two children, feel cheated if either or both marry way outside their culture and faith and often break off relationships creating a chasm of unhappiness between the two generations.

Though Bollywood has any number of examples of 'happily married' inter-religion couples, Indian society as a whole, according to social observers, has yet to truly accept inter-religious marriages.

In India, parents, however progressive, look to their children as the 'support' of their old age. They hope for continuity in religious celebrations, cultural harmony and a stress-free life when they stake all they have to educate and provide everything to their children. "It all depends upon what kind of bride comes into the family. She can break or make a family," says Shobha Jain, wife of an industrialist. "In our case, things are truly sad.

"We are a Jain family that lives on three floors of our bungalow in South Mumbai. The three brothers—my husband and two others—and their families had a common kitchen and celebrated festivals, parties and family occasions together. Now each young son has married either a Muslim or Christian bride. The result is that non-vegetarian food is cooked by them in kitchens which are now separate. The young daughters-in-law do not attend our religious or cultural get-togethers saying their religions do not permit them to do so. The happiness of the whole family is destroyed."

A Recent Celebrity Mixed Marriage

The most recent couple to hit mixed-marriage headlines comprises cricketer Zaheer Khan and his girlfriend Isha Sharvani. While Zaheer is a Muslim, Isha Sharvani is the daughter of dancer Daksha Seth and Vissaro, an Australian composer. Born in 1984, Isha is an expert in yoga, dance and martial arts and lives in an ashram in Kerala. She has worked in films, among which is Subhash Ghai's *Kisna: The Warrior Poet*. Zaheer hit headlines as the leading wicket-taker in the World Cup in 2011. The two met in 2005 and over a period of time, despite several differences, have decided to tie the knot later this year. They will be one more successful couple if they build a strong marriage.

"A major reason why families do not like mixing religions through the marriages of their sons or daughters is that in India, property, marriage and child custody laws are different for each religious group," says Ankit Talwar, a lawyer. "The Hindu Code Bill applies to all Indic religions though local customs may vary. Hinduism, Sikhism, Jainism and Buddhism have the same foundation of beliefs. Personal laws for Muslims and Christians are different. So when the only son or daughter of a family marries outside his religion, the parents are concerned about his being the heir not only to their family responsibilities but also to their way of life and assets.

"Tap any parent in India and most will say that they would prefer their sons and daughters to marry any community within the religious commonality so that adjustments are easier. Of course, finally, the nature and willingness to adjust by both parties decides whether the family and the new couple will be happy together. Even in the West, psychiatrists realise today that young people who 'have not made peace with their parents' cannot make a success of any relationship! Their guilt at alienating them is more in Indian society where parents are considered equal to God. Indian laws also demand that children should look after their elderly parents by supporting them. Their monetary help to their parents is tax-free unlike in other countries. This is the culture of India and it cannot be wiped out."

"I was brought up as a devout Hindu," says Srilata Ghosh, a successful doctor. "And I am proud of my heritage. I love the beauty of my culture. I think every person has the right to be proud of his or her culture and religion. In India, religion is not limited to temples, mosques, churches or the act of praying or worship. It influences our food, relationships, apparel, language, festivals, sacraments, pilgrimages and even the way we look at the world.

"Experts like Neil MacGregor, director of the British Museum, have said that Indian thought and life even today connects to the edicts of Emperor Ashoka from 236 BC. Ours is one of the oldest cultures of the world. More than 90 per cent of Indians are profoundly religious. When two people have a totally different upbringing, how can they find peace together unless both give up their ways of life and create a third one successfully? Minor differences can be ironed out but major ones cause disaster after the first flush of romance has waned."

"Tap any parent in India and most will say that they would prefer their sons and daughters to marry any community within the religious commonality so that adjustments are easier."

Pooja Bedi sums up the debate, "If for any reason a young woman or man feels that his/her parents could oppose the marriage, he/she must figure out whether he/she is open to a life without the parents' blessings and to handling the worst possible scenario after the honey-and-roses romance is over!"

Jordanian Women in Mixed Marriages Face Legal Discrimination

Laurent Zecchini

Laurent Zecchini is a reporter for Le Monde. *In the following viewpoint, he reports that women in Jordan who marry foreigners are faced with legal and social discrimination. In particular, Jordanian law dictates that women in such unions cannot pass on Jordanian nationality to their husbands and children, which prevents them from having any rights under the law. Zecchini points out that the law is different for Jordanian men. He also notes that the government justifies the law by arguing that it cannot afford to offer citizenship to foreign husbands and children, but critics contend that such reasoning is only a distraction from Jordan's chauvinistic legal system.*

As you read, consider the following questions:

1. How many Palestinian refugees live in Jordan, according to the author?
2. According to Jordan's Interior Ministry, how many women are affected by the country's legal discrimination against mixed marriages?

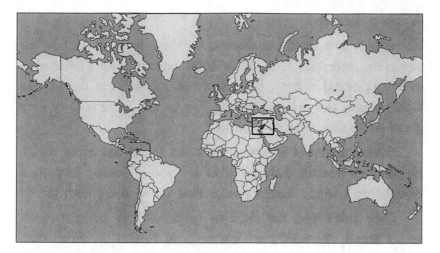

3. How many women and children does the Interior Ministry estimate these repressive laws affect?

"Everyone has the right to a nationality," says the 15th article of the Universal Declaration of Human Rights. Nima Habashney, who lives in Jordan, does not believe in this right anymore. In Jordan's Hashemite Kingdom, women married to foreigners cannot pass on Jordanian nationality to their husbands and children.

Legally speaking, their children and husbands do not exist—even if they've been living in Jordan all their life. They are tolerated, but they don't have any papers or social rights, making them more vulnerable than the nearly one million Palestinian refugees who live in Jordan with the United Nations' help.

It works differently for Jordanian men. The foreign wives and children of Jordanian men automatically receive citizenship. The law also stipulates that the children of a male Jordanian inherit their father's nationality no matter where they were born, even if they've never set foot in Jordan.

A Long Battle

Habashney is a small but fearless woman. Born in Jordan, she began an uncertain struggle in 2004 against male domination in a very tribal society. She launched a campaign for human rights under the motto "We can live in the same society even if we don't share the same ideas."

Having married a Moroccan man (who has since died), Habashney has six children who are today denied Jordanian citizenship and the basic benefits that come along with it.

They don't have the right to work, to rent an apartment, or to access the public education and health systems. They cannot have a driver's license and do not enjoy basic civil rights.

For Habashney, her children's missing citizenship status has meant a lifetime of hurdles: in police stations, schools, health centers, public service bureaus. Everywhere, she wrestles with unsympathetic and sometimes aggressive civil servants. "Why did you marry a foreigner? You've made a big mistake, now you have to pay for it," they respond to her queries.

A Widespread Problem

But Habashney understood that she was not the only Jordanian woman living with the same mix of ostracism, sexual discrimination and xenophobia. Indeed, it turns out there are nearly 66,000 women in the same situation, according to Jordan's Interior Ministry. Jordanian families have an average of 5.4 children, meaning overall the country's discriminatory citizenship laws could be affecting more than 350,000 people.

The scope of the situation may be exactly why the government has the laws it does. Jordan, a small country of 6.4 million people who are mostly of Palestinian descent, cannot afford to welcome so many new citizens. Habashney agrees that while Jordan's feudal and chauvinist structure are largely to blame for her family's stateless condition, demographic considerations influence government policy as well.

Others, however, accuse the government of exaggerating statistics in order to justify its arbitrary citizen laws. Interestingly enough, there were only 16,000 women officially in Habashney's situation in 2004.

In 2002, Jordan's Queen Rania announced that the government was considering giving Jordan women the right to pass their nationality to their children. But the move provoked an outcry among tribes who are the backbone of the Jordan monarchy.

"It's a human rights and discrimination issue, not a political issue," says Nermeen Murad, who heads the information center of Jordan's King Hussein Foundation, a humanitarian organization.

And the Queen?

The government claims that most women in Habashney's situation are married to Palestinians, who—if they were allowed Jordanian citizenship—would be all the more encouraged to flee Gaza or the West Bank of the Jordan River. In many cases, says Habashney, Palestinians actually defend the law. "They tell me: 'By emptying Palestine, you play Israel's game,'" she says. Never mind that most foreign husbands of Jordanian women are actually Egyptian.

In 2002, Jordan's Queen Rania announced that the government was considering giving Jordan women the right to pass their nationality to their children. But the move provoked an outcry among tribes who are the backbone of the Jordan monarchy. An amendment was published to make people forget the incident, but it was too late, and since then, the Transjordanians (those born in Jordan of Jordan extraction) grew more suspicious of the queen, who is of Palestinian descent.

Jordan's complicated relationship vis-à-vis Palestine, it seems, is the real stumbling block. Since 2003, several ministers have stated that the issue of Jordanian women married to foreigners will evaporate once the Israeli-Palestinian conflict is resolved. Habashney isn't willing to wait.

"The Palestinian issue is not my problem. I worry about our kids who have no present and no future in this country," says Habashney. "We won't remain silent. We're going to speak and to demonstrate, we'll keep fighting."

Bosnia and Herzegovina's Sectarian Divide Is Influencing Interfaith Marriage Rates

Damir Dizdarević

Damir Dizdarević is a contributor to the Pescanik website. In the following viewpoint, he reveals that he is thinking about leaving his hometown of Sarajevo, the capital city of Bosnia and Herzegovina, because of rising religious and sectarian tensions. Dizdarević maintains that with growing opposition to mixed marriage, he and his family do not feel welcome anymore. He sees this as part of a larger trend, in which religion is more valued than education and culture. In the past, Sarajevo was proud of its multicultural demographics and was open and accepting to people no matter of religion; but since the war in Bosnia, he believes that religious elements have taken control and seek to marginalize atheists and those of other religions.

As you read, consider the following questions:

1. How did Deputy Reis describe atheists in a recent interview in the newspaper *Dnevni Avaz*?
2. According to the author, what did Emir Suljagic try to do for atheist and nonreligious students?

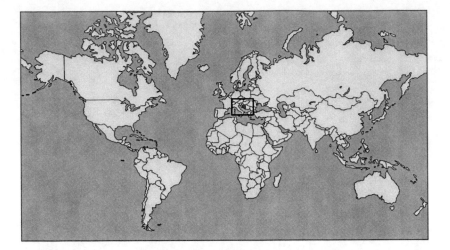

3. What cultural institution in Sarajevo does the author report is holding barely one concert a month because of the rise of religious entertainment?

I'm thinking about leaving my city of Sarajevo. I've been thinking about this for some time, as have probably many Sarajevo citizens faced with a similar situation. I am not materially deprived and I would not be leaving because of economic reasons. Moreover there is no war, at least not the type waged by guns. No one is forcing us to leave either. However, my family and I do not feel welcome anymore in the city where we were born. This city has nothing further to offer. With a dire need to have everything nationally labelled, the majority refers to us as "mixed marriage". The term "mixed" I can only understand in the context of different sexes, but obviously this is not what others have in mind. The idiom— mixed marriage—which may to some mean nothing, to others means everything. In the most recent history of Bosnia and Herzegovina, it was much exploited in various, predominantly negative ways. In the former Yugoslavia, mixed marriages were highly encouraged and symbolized the foundation of brotherhood and unity of nations and nationalities, but soon after the beginning of the war they grew to be the most unacceptable social category, with children from such marriages becoming particularly unacceptable. These are the people who do not have "their own", meaning that everyone else who does (have "their own") rejects them. Therefore it is not surprising that many people from this social category left the former Yugoslavia, and BIH [Bosnia and Herzegovina] in particular, since most of them lived there. And since all the governments in BIH since 1992 were mostly nationalistic, they made special efforts to further complicate the life of these people and in a "nice way" hint that it's better for them to leave. Because with such people it's never certain. One is never sure who they will vote for, and one cannot truly rely on them.

A Deplorable Campaign

At the beginning of and during the war, a few high-ranking Bosnian officials publicly declared children from mixed marriages to be genetic waste. They even had a bizarre "scientific" explanation for this, which ... made things even more deplorable. On several occasions, after the war, the Islamic community targeted "those who were raised in atheism," which in the majority of cases stood for those who came from households comprising several nationalities/religions, or those who never gave religion any particular significance. Most recently the deputy reis, in an interview to the daily newspaper [Dnevni] Avaz on the occasion of Eid [Eid al-Fitr, a Muslim holiday], described such people as "the most dangerous enemies". I must admit that it's an extraordinary feeling to read in the largest Bosnian daily newspaper that, overnight, I became someone's greatest enemy, even though I was born, lived and survived here. The title of the interview (if I remember correctly) was "Muslims are once again under the yoke of tyranny", and the part about the enemy was emphasized with a separate text box. Considering that most people who read

[Dnevni] Avaz read only headlines, subheadings, and eventually text boxes, it is not difficult to make out the intent of the article. But there's more.

It is well known that religion, education and culture constantly overlap and pressure each other. At some point of life, this mystic triangle is something almost every person encounters. Some less, some more. The mutual relationship between these three categories, similar to conflicts in this region, is perhaps more intense than anywhere else. During the time of our history marked as "Tito's Yugoslavia" [referring to Josip Broz Tito, president of Yugoslavia from 1953–1980], education and culture had priority over religion. Or, perhaps it's better to say that religion had less influence on education and culture. Today, things are exactly the opposite. Religion rules, so not much else exists for people who can't identify themselves with it, since education and culture are in a free fall (to put it mildly).

Institutions under threat of collapsing or those that have already closed are precisely the institutions that support the cultural, multiethnic character of Sarajevo and its diverse history.

An Unfortunate Controversy

One very interesting and painfully clear example of the supremacy of religion over education was the series of events relating to Emir Suljagic, the (former) minister of education of the Sarajevo Canton. Contrary to other politicians, he belongs to a group of atypical individuals who tried to do something for children that come from families in which religion and religious identity is a matter of choice rather than an obligation. He wanted to make them equal with others, because they were not, despite the claims of authorities that Sarajevo is a multiethnic city and a symbol of tolerance. The fury over the now former minister's decision to make religious classes an elective (with free choice being an underlying principle), and not include them in the average score calculation, so that those who do not take the elective are not sanctioned, is unprecedented. Religious circles, spearheaded by the Islamic community and followed by the representatives of other "constituent" religions, used all possible means to threaten him with basically everything. They of course mentioned Srebrenica [referring to a massacre in July of 1995, during which more than eight thousand Bosnian Muslims were killed], because this argument can be taken whenever there is a lack of any other. The frightening campaign, framed in the context of the Srebrenica genocide, as insane as it may sound, was completely based on fabrications. They argued that the minister wants to abolish religious education, which was never the case. Even today you can find all articles from that era and see that there is not one document, statement, or anything else that came from the Ministry of Education, which referred to the abolition of religion. The intent was just to allow a freedom of choice: religious education for those who are interested, as well as the right to opt out and not be discriminated for it.

Despite the unprecedentedly brutal attacks, the minister remained adamant, and resigned (for the first time). It became very obvious that he was left without any real support. His party reluctantly stood behind him, the Cantonal Assembly passed some sort of decision that softened the statement originally issued by the minister, and it did not accept his resignation. 1:0 for religion. Despite numerous tangible successes, I believe that Suljagic will not be remembered for anything besides his false "abolition of religious education". And there were many things that the minister of education accomplished in a very short time frame, which is best demonstrated by the public support received from teachers after his second, irrevocable resignation. But the article is not about this.

The Establishment of Bosnia and Herzegovina

Following the Great War [World War I], Bosnia became part of the South Slav state of Yugoslavia, only to be given to the Nazi puppet state, the Independent State of Croatia (NDH) during World War II. . . . The end of the war saw the establishment of a Communist, federal Yugoslavia under wartime leader Josip Broz Tito, with Bosnia and Herzegovina as one of six republics in the Yugoslav federation.

After Tito died in 1980, Yugoslavia's unraveling was hastened by Slobodan Milosevic's rise to power in 1986. . . . By late September 1991, Bosnian Serb Radovan Karadzic's Serbian Democratic Party (SDS) had declared four self-proclaimed "Serb Autonomous Regions (SAO)" in Bosnia. In October 1991, the Bosnian Serbs announced the formation within Bosnia of a "Serbian Republic of Bosnia-Herzegovina" that would have its own constitution and parliamentary assembly. In January 1992, Radovan Karadzic publicly proclaimed a fully independent "Republic of the Serbian People in Bosnia-Herzegovina." On March 1, 1992, the Bosnian government held a referendum on independence. Bosnia's parliament declared the republic's independence on April 5, 1992. However, this move was opposed by Serb representatives, who had voted in their own referendum in November 1991 in favor of remaining in Yugoslavia. Bosnian Serbs, supported by neighboring Serbia, responded with armed force in an effort to partition the republic along ethnic lines. Recognition of Bosnia and Herzegovina's independence by the United States and the European community occurred on April 6–7, and Bosnia and Herzegovina was admitted to the United Nations on May 22, 1992.

"Background Notes: Bosnia and Herzegovina,"
US State Department, March 14, 2012.

Today's Sarajevo

The provided example clearly shows the superiority of religion over education in today's Sarajevo. Also, it demonstrates what happens when those who are "multi" in multiethnic Sarajevo try to stand for something or someone supporting or representing multiethnic interests. The bullet that was mailed to Suljagic was not addressed only to him, but also to all those who believe that he was doing something which would bring true equality, at least in the area of education. And even if the bullet could be interpreted as an act of a sole extremist, the recent general and media campaigns to which Suljagic was subjected certainly are not. The bullet is just a logical sequence in the chain of events already witnessed in other former Yugoslav countries. For example, hypocritical use of compelling arguments based on surveys each time "multi" should be put into practice. Like, let's interview children and parents and see if they would like to exclude a religion course with a 95% score average from the overall grade average—and then argue that the majority is for religious education. Well of course it is, when this is the best way for students to improve their overall grade average. I guarantee that, if a same survey was conducted on the theme "do you want the marks in mathematics to be removed from the average grade score", support would be even more overwhelming than for religious education. However, such a survey would be qualified as unreasonable (and it would be).

After 36 years of life in Sarajevo and believing to be an open-minded person, for a while now I have been wondering how much time must pass in order to, once more, witness a redistribution of power between religion, culture and education.

The dominance of religion over culture is also very visible. In Sarajevo, mosques are rapidly being built on every piece of unused land. Before someone accuses me in advance of being against mosques, I must say that I am not. I grew up in a city full of mosques from the time of the Ottoman Empire and many of them I highly appreciate as cultural and historical monuments as well as religious shrines. But the flood of newly built mosques, which are very difficult to relate to the ones built a long time ago, is very indicative. At the same time, museums and art galleries are being closed down, theatres only play several shows per month, and the Sarajevo Philharmonic Orchestra barely holds one concert every month. At the same time, manifestations of religious character can without trouble fill the Zetra [Zetra Olympic Hall], while a prime cultural event is denoted by an Angelina Jolie movie. Institutions under threat of collapsing or those that have already closed are precisely the institutions that support the cultural, multiethnic character of Sarajevo and its diverse history. One cannot say that religious communities are directly responsible for the collapse of culture, or that they should have to financially support cultural institutions, but, without a doubt, they did attract the "audience" to their side, which eventually led to abandoning other types of cultural events.

The Future

If one adds the extremely poor state support for cultural and historical institutions, it is clear where this is leading us. To again have a culture that once existed in Sarajevo in an environment where religion is omnipresent will require a strong state which, unfortunately, Bosnia is not today. Information about the deterioration of culture and education catch media interest very briefly, if at all. Very few people, generally those that have no influence, react to such news. Not one religious community reacts to these things, because they do not need any museums, or galleries, or concerts. Because they know that those who visit such sites are not suitable material for processing and indoctrination.

After 36 years of life in Sarajevo and believing to be an open-minded person, for a while now I have been wondering how much time must pass in order to, once more, witness a redistribution of power between religion, culture and education. And how much time must pass so that my Sarajevo again understands the meaning of multiethnicity, diversity and acceptance of others. Some 20 years ago this seemed to be clear to everyone. Maybe it was clear to those who no longer live in this city, who were killed, died or left. For the citizens of Sarajevo today that idea, unfortunately, seems to be far from comprehensible, although I believe that almost everyone is ready to swear to the multiethnic character of the city, without thinking about what Sarajevo can offer to those for whom religion is not the most important thing. Declarative multiethnicity is much more hypocritical than recognizing Sarajevo as a city with a majority of Muslim population, and that it is within this context that it develops and operates. Sometimes I truly believe that it would, for the rest of us, be better if that was the case, because every society that has a defined majority will also have a minority that has its distinct rights. In the case of Sarajevo today, theoretical multiethnicity actually allows the majority to do whatever it wants, while completely marginalizing minorities.

And lastly, there is a problem of extremely twisted criteria by which standards are being set. If someone today tells a non-Bosnian that people living in Sarajevo are not doing well, they will probably get a typical response such as "so what is it that they lack, no one is lifting a finger against them". True, but this lack of direct threat is far from enough to make someone feel good. The siege of Sarajevo and rivers of blood that flowed through the streets of this city have made people react only to life-threatening things. Everything else is fine. I survived the whole war in Sarajevo, and experienced many unpleasant things without contributing to any of them, and yet 17 years after the war I cannot console myself with the sentence "all is good, just as long as there is no shooting". I want to see that my city accepts and wants me as its citizen, and that it is able to offer me something beyond physical protection. In my city I wish to feel like a citizen of Europe and not only and exclusively as "other" (since I am not a member of one of BIH's constituent peoples). For anyone to feel like a citizen of the world in today's Sarajevo requires much more than providing just plain material security.

Tribal Fighting Frightens Kenya's "Mixed" Couples

Shashank Bengali

Shashank Bengali is a reporter for the Los Angeles Times. *In the following viewpoint, he examines the rising conflicts between tribal groups in Kenya that have affected many intertribal marriages. Bengali reports that in the aftermath of a controversial 2007 national election, long-simmering tribal rivalries between the country's forty-two ethnic groups erupted in violence that left many dead. He also notes that these tensions threaten the tolerant and cosmopolitan city of Nairobi as well as generate resentment and discrimination against mixed-tribe marriages.*

As you read, consider the following questions:

1. According to the author, how many Kenyans were killed in intertribal violence between December 2007 and February 2008?

2. What ethnic group is predominant in business and politics in Kenya?

3. According to a national survey conducted by the Steadman polling firm, how many Kenyans would consider intertribal marriage?

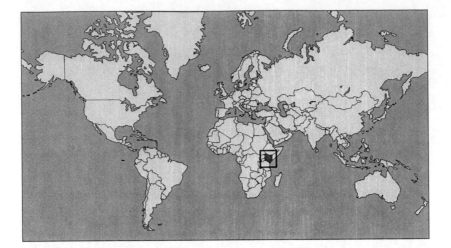

In the six weeks that intertribal fighting has ripped through Kenya, Josphat Karanja hasn't once called his father, not even after clashes erupted near the family home in the turbulent Rift Valley.

"I know what he's going to say," said Karanja, a 30-year-old computer systems manager. "I can't hear that right now."

Karanja is a Kikuyu, the dominant tribe in Kenya. Three years ago, against his father's wishes, he married a woman from the smaller Luo community, Everlyn Adoyo, whom he'd courted by showing up at her home unannounced almost every day for several months until she agreed to go out with him.

Today the couple is the picture of wedded bliss: she a bubbly salesclerk, he a straight-faced techie with a wry sense of humor. But to the chagrin of Karanja's father, their tribes are on opposite sides of Kenya's bloody post-election divide, which has pit supporters of President Mwai Kibaki, a Kikuyu, against those who back the Luo opposition leader, Raila Odinga.

Mixed couples such as Karanja and Adoyo are a symbol of modern, cosmopolitan Kenya, which until recently was an island of stability in East Africa. But the violence that's killed more than 1,000 people since December has proved that for all of the country's progress, tribe still matters in Kenya.

In recent years, with Kenyans from all over the country flocking to the capital, Nairobi, tribal identities have blurred and mixed marriages no longer are uncommon.

The controversial election, which independent observers say Kibaki stole, has reopened generations-old rivalries among Kenya's 42 ethnic groups. Perhaps none is more fierce than that between Kikuyus, who've dominated business and politics since the country won its independence in 1963, and Luos, who wear their long exclusion from power like a giant chip on the shoulder.

In recent years, with Kenyans from all over the country flocking to the capital, Nairobi, tribal identities have blurred and mixed marriages no longer are uncommon. In a national survey last year by the Steadman polling firm, 3 out of 4 Kenyans said they'd consider marrying outside their tribes.

But in a reflection of the deep mistrust between their communities, Kikuyus and Luos were the least likely of the major tribes to want to intermarry.

"I feel proud that I've married outside my tribe. It's something exotic," said Karanja, sipping coffee at an outdoor cafe with Adoyo, 25, smiling back at him. "But now I feel that people will think twice about marrying someone from another group."

In their concrete block of comfortable apartments in Kinoo (pronounced "kin-OH"), a bedroom community 20 minutes outside Nairobi, the couple lives among middle-class Kenyans of many different groups, bonding in the evenings over shared interests such as English Premier League soccer.

Before the election, politics was merely a diversion. Despite the fact that they supported rival presidential candidates,

---

Kenya's Ethnic and Religious Composition

Population
37 million (2007 est.)

Government
Republic since independence in 1963.

Ethnicity
More than 70 tribal groups exist;
largest groups:
• Kikuyu, 22%
• Luhya, 14%
• Luo, 13%

Religion
• Christian, 78%
• Muslim, 10%
• Other, 12%

TAKEN FROM: *CIA World Factbook* (U.S.), ESRI, 2007.

Karanja—who voted for Kibaki—brought home Odinga posters as a gesture of domestic bipartisanship.

Now they fear for their multiethnic oasis.

One recent evening, in a shantytown a few hundred yards from their building, a group of young Kikuyu men torched a line of tin shacks belonging to Luos. Soon after that, a mixed couple in a neighboring apartment moved out because the man—a Kalenjin, another tribe that's fought Kikuyus—worried that the mobs would come for him next.

The mood among their neighbors has darkened. "There is a lot of careless talking," Adoyo said. Once they dropped in on a Kikuyu neighbor upstairs and the conversation turned to a recent spate of attacks on Luos in the western town of Nakuru.

"Let those Luos be killed," Adoyo recalled the neighbor saying, as she sat in his living room stone-faced. "Let them be disciplined."

Adoyo was raised in Nairobi, and her family didn't have a problem with her marrying a non-Luo man. One close cousin married a Kalenjin, another a European. "As long as he doesn't beat you, and you are happy," Adoyo's father said to her when she and Karanja were married.

It was his parents, who live in a village near Nakuru, who were wary. "The first thing they asked me was, 'Why do you marry a Luo?'" Karanja recalled. "My only answer was, 'Why not?' I like the person."

His father never came to terms with the union, and it's badly strained their relationship. These days, when he wants news from home, Karanja calls his brother to make sure their parents are OK.

In Nairobi, they said, communities seemed to mix easily enough. Adoyo works for a Kikuyu who owns several cell phone outlets, and at nights she attends college classes in human resources management. When the new semester started a few weeks ago, however, she was disturbed when she introduced herself by her nickname, Eva, and classmates shot back: "Eva what?" They wanted to know her family name—the easiest indicator of one's tribe.

"That never happened before," she said. "But now I always hear people saying, 'Kabila gani?'"—Swahili for "Which tribe?"

So they've reluctantly begun looking for a new home in a safe section of Nairobi, where Adoyo's sister lives. Karanja is due to complete his master's degree in information technology in April, and he plans to apply to PhD programs overseas.

"I always thought I would do that at some point," he said. "Now seems to be the time. I don't think there's a bright future in Kenya."

Intertribal Marriages in Africa Are Stigmatized

Melinda Ozongwu

Melinda Ozongwu is a journalist. In the following viewpoint, she discusses the stigma of interracial and intertribal marriages in Africa. Ozongwu argues that history, cultural stereotypes, and long-standing intertribal conflicts affect the perception of mixed marriages in most African countries. Another problem is that tribal identity is so important in African society that marrying outside of it leads many to view such marriages as a betrayal. Ozongwu concludes that even modern and cosmopolitan Africans are impacted by such factors when it comes to mixed couples.

As you read, consider the following questions:

1. What factor does the author believe is important in the response to mixed couples?

2. According to the author, what do some traditionalists believe is preferable to intertribal marriage?

3. What does the author cite as the stereotype of African women marrying white men?

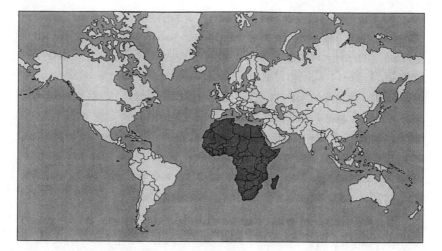

It may seem odd to be discussing the taboo of interracial or inter-tribal relationships in 2012, but though everyone is now supposed to be totally relaxed about "mixed couples", there are still combinations that make some outwardly enlightened people uncomfortable for reasons cultural, religious, or other.

Our identity often sets parameters for our choices, parameters that are set by what we feel is appropriate based on where we come from and what we believe in even if we don't realise we believe in anything at all. True, younger generations are steered towards greater tolerance, open-mindedness and acceptance of difference than the generations that preceded them. They are guided to believe that race, sexuality, religion and tradition are personal matters, not subject to the judgment of others. That's the ideal, but judgment by others isn't easy to escape, or entirely withstand, in practice.

Mixed Couples and Context

It is hard not to have some sort of reaction when you see an interracial couple. The reaction need not be negative; it may simply be one of observation, that you notice the couple because they are not of the same race. Nonetheless, noticing the couple for that reason isn't neutral. I believe setting or context plays a very big role in the response to or interpretation of a mixed couple. When I walk the streets of London, for example, I don't think I'm as observant of interracial couples, probably because interracial dating/marriage is so common. But when I see a "mixed" couple in Uganda or any other African country, I do more than just observe. I form an opinion, and the opinion has more dimension to it than just my awareness of noticing. The opinion is affected by my own culture and traditions, which do include stereotypes.

We are familiar with the worldwide definition of an interracial couple, but perhaps not so much with inter-tribal. It simply means two people from different tribes getting involved in a relationship, or getting married. Doesn't sound like a big deal, but they might speak different languages (though they'll probably have one language in common), have different belief systems, and be accustomed to different kinds of traditional dishes.

Betrayal

While it has become increasingly common for people to marry outside their tribes, it isn't a preferable option for traditionalists. I was once told by someone whom I would describe as a devoted traditionalist that instead of marrying a man from my country but of a different tribe, it would be far more acceptable to marry a man from an entirely different country altogether. Inter-tribal conflicts, stereotypes and history can make it hard for some inter-tribal relationships to enjoy immunity from judgment. The idea of someone marrying outside their tribe leaves some people feeling that their customs, values and traditions are being betrayed, that should a woman date or marry a man from a different tribe it gives superiority to that man's tribe, an affirmation that her own tribe wasn't good enough. If a man marries a woman outside of his tribe, it's because he thinks his "own" women are not beautiful enough. People feel betrayed, which is interesting because while everyone else is feeling betrayed, no one considers the sense of betrayal those in the relationship must be feeling.

In this respect, when discussing inter-tribal relationships and the stigma and stereotypes that come with them, Africans can come out sounding a bit backward, but our tribes are part of our heritage; they are important. A lot of Africans value their sense of tribal belonging as much as they do nationality or religion. Of course the degree to which this is so varies from one person to the next, but "tradition" has a way of surprising even the most "modern" of Africans.

We are familiar with the worldwide definition of an interracial couple, but perhaps not so much with inter-tribal. It simply means two people from different tribes getting involved in a relationship, or getting married.

Mixed Marriage in Africa

Interracial relationships exist in Africa, too. They may be few and far between, but as our countries continue to attract international investments and businesses, the expat communities will continue to grow and interracial relationships will increase in tandem. In my country, the main stigma of interracial relationships is money. People assume that the black woman must be with the white man for money, they assume that the black man must be with the white woman for money—money, green cards, financial security, light-skinned babies, the list of "reasons" are many, and there are examples that confirm the assumptions. They might be the exceptions, but that can't offer much comfort to other interracial couples. It can't be easy walking down the street hand in hand with your white partner, knowing almost everyone assumes you're a prostitute or a gold digger. In Africa, interracial relationships are constantly judged and observed, and I can see no other solution to this problem than time and numbers. I suppose, looking on the bright side, at least no one is being stoned or killed for dating a white man or woman. Idle gossip and awkward stares is surely something most people can manage.

I haven't played by all of the "rules" but I know those who have. Some people are more comfortable with the familiar, the acceptable, the "right" way of doing things and would never consider an inter-tribal relationship. Others make their choice regardless of tribal affiliations or what's "right". Neither is without its burdens.

Russia's Mixed Marriages Are Endangered by Cultural and Religious Pressures

Andrei Zolotov Jr.

Andrei Zolotov Jr. is a journalist and founding editor of Russia Profile. In the following viewpoint, he surveys the state of mixed marriage in Russia, finding they are less common in areas of the country marked by high levels of ethnic tension and are more prevalent in areas where religion is not widely practiced. Zolotov reports that the subject of marriage between Christians and Muslims is very controversial across the country and is hotly debated on Internet forums. Almost every major religion in Russia has come out against interreligious marriages, a controversial subject because it involves the issue of conversion. For many Russian women, Muslim men are prospective marriage partners because they offer a traditionalist appeal and do not drink alcohol.

As you read, consider the following questions:

1. According to the author, in what part of Russia are interreligious marriages on the decline?
2. What Russian Orthodox missionary has a "scientific" explanation against mixed marriages for Russians?

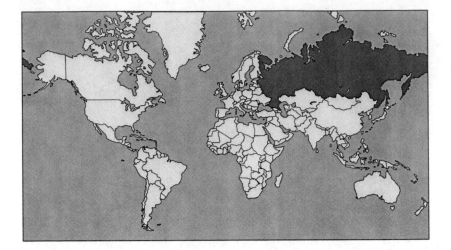

3. What percentage of marriages in Tatarstan are mixed unions, according to Guzel Stolyarova?

From the age of 16 to the age of 20, Lidia Korneva travelled the world working as a model. Shortly before leaving home she was baptized in the Orthodox Church—"to stay safe and sound"—but remained largely a nominal Christian. While many of her colleagues married foreigners, she eventually returned to Moscow and worked as a successful fashion journalist. Now, at the age of 30, she has been married to an Uzbek businessman for seven years. Her husband is 18 years her senior, has lived in Moscow since 1991, has children with his first Russian wife and, according to Lidia, is now taking an increasingly profound interest in his religion, Islam. "We are a very successful example of a mixed marriage," Korneva said. "I remember that he is Uzbek only when he speaks to his relatives on the phone or when we visit Uzbekistan."

She also realizes that he is Muslim when she cooks him breakfast before dawn during the fasting month of Ramadan and the special dinner she makes him at the end of it so that he "comes out of the fast fine." She also covers her head and wears long sleeves during their trips to Uzbekistan. For now, Korneva's husband is only planning to pray five times a day.

They had a Muslim wedding—nikah—but decided, by mutual consent, to hush up—or lie—about the question of whether she was Muslim. For now Korneva has not changed her faith. But she does not rule out the possibility of eventually converting to Islam. Overall, she said, her experience with Islam has so far been largely positive, and with Christianity—largely negative.

And what about children? Are they going to be Russian or Uzbek, Christian or Muslim? They do not have children yet, and "we will tackle problems as they emerge," Korneva said.

A Mixed Blessing

Mixed marriages have long been a part of Russian life. Marriages between members of different Christian denominations were heavily regulated in prerevolutionary Russia, although some unions of this kind were possible from the 18th century onward. Interreligious marriages were banned because religions do not accept them—and family law in Imperial Russia was defined by the respective religions that the government recognized.

In Soviet times, while marriages with foreign nationals were for the most part prohibited, marital unions between representatives of the Soviet Union's hundreds of ethnicities were hailed as an embodiment of the new Soviet nation and as liberation from the shackles of religion. According to Valery Tishkov, the director of the Institute of Ethnology and Anthropology of the Russian Academy of Sciences, about one-third of Russians were born into mixed families, which is why he argues in favor of introducing dual ethnic identity in the country.

In post-Soviet Russia the emergence of nationalist movements and the religious revival has provoked strong criticism of mixed marriages among traditionalists, as well as an expectation that their numbers would go down.

They do indeed appear to be down in the North Caucasus—a part of the country marked by particular ethnic tension. But the share of mixed marriages continues to grow in Tatarstan despite expectations to the contrary. The trend appears to be the same in other ethnically mixed areas of the Volga Region, as well as in Moscow, St. Petersburg and other big cities, although there is precious little solid research available in this delicate field, said Guzel Stolyarova, a professor of ethnography at the Kazan Federal University who has researched mixed marriages in Tatarstan.

Mixed marriages have long been a part of Russian life.

On the other hand, the subject of mixed marriages, particularly those between Christians and Muslims, is being widely debated in the media and in private conversations, but most hotly—on Internet forums.

Typing Out Feelings

"Traditions should always take precedence," wrote Zaur Davdiev on a Caucasus Internet forum. "Once we've lost them we will lose our cultural values and the uniqueness of our people. I fell in love with a Russian girl—so what? No matter how painful it is, I would never trample my culture—the more so because she has grown up according to other standards, and what is normal for me is outrageous for her and vice versa."

Other users argue that it is fine to marry someone of another nationality, as long as both spouses are Muslim, or that it is fine for a man to marry a woman of another ethnicity or even religion, because a man can "convert" his wife, while it is wrong for a woman to marry out of her culture. "I think that a man can marry a girl of any ethnicity, because in any case, if he is a man who keeps his customs and traditions and knows his language, he will make her—if he is a Chechen—a Chechen, if he is Ossetian—Ossetian. I know men from the Caucasus who married Russians and these girls were no different from the locals," wrote Iman Chichieva.

A user named Irina Kartmazova argues: "If it turns out that I marry a Russian, will I automatically become Russian? That's ridiculous. I will never change my name, religion, my interests, even for the sake of a husband, no matter what ethnicity he is. And the children will know the customs of both their father and my people." And another user by the name of Rosita Rosy Urumyants simply wrote: "Marry for love."

The privacy and facelessness afforded by an Internet discussion is probably most fitting for these private, loaded issues. But even in Internet forums, people prefer to speak about abstract concepts rather than personal experience. It is still harder to find people to be interviewed about their experience of mixed marriage—the ones who agree to belong to the urban, secularized intelligentsia.

Sermons and Critiques

Preachers and authorities of pretty much every religion in Russia have spoken out against mixed marriages in recent years. The subject of mixed marriages is most divisive in relations between the Russian Orthodox Church and the Islamic establishment in Russia, which are characterized by proclamations of religious peace on the official level but are in reality much more complicated due to the taboo issue of conversion.

The ethnic factor is secondary when it comes to divorce.

Daniel Sysoev, an Orthodox priest and missionary who was murdered in his church on the outskirts of Moscow in November of 2009, was himself half-Russian and half-Tatar. He was known as an active missionary trying to convert Muslims—a policy which church authorities prefer to avoid and for which he was strongly criticized by Muslims and by some

Christians. One of his brochures was titled "Marriage with a Muslim" and argued against intermarriage, using church rules, anecdotal evidence and widely held beliefs about the position of a woman in an Islamic family. Another prominent—and much more "mainstream"—Orthodox missionary, Archdeacon Andrei Kurayev, also actively argues against mixed marriage, including its purely racial aspect or losing the Russian "recessive gene" to the stronger Caucasian or central Asian ones. "Yes, it has happened that the unbelieving husband was sanctified through his believing wife," he said in an interview referring to the Corinthians 1 7:14. "And that the husband and children converted through a Christian wife. But that was the case when our faith was strong. Today in such marriages the Russian woman is the weak side. She herself does not know her faith."

The subject of mixed marriages is most divisive in relations between the Russian Orthodox Church and the Islamic establishment in Russia.

Interestingly enough, all opponents of mixed marriages tend to present their own side as weaker and the "other" as stronger. Tatar historian Rafik Mukhametshin, the rector of the [Russian] Islamic University in Kazan, said that according to his observations, when it comes to the upbringing of children, the female side of the family is stronger. "If the mother is Russian, children are more likely to be Russian," Mukhametshin said. "There are exceptions, of course." He added that he has a "mixed attitude toward mixed marriages." "On the one hand, it signifies a modern trend of integration, it is inevitable in the conditions of globalization.

"But on the other hand, no matter how much we say that the family is based on love and mutual respect, the problem of national identity doesn't disappear. Maybe at some point everybody is happy, but as people get older, maybe in the second half of family life, the identity problem shows up anyway. People start remembering their roots—one is Russian, the other Tatar; one drawn to the mosque, and the other to the church. And these problems appear inevitably."

Mukhametshin recalled a recent case, when a baby died in a young Tatar-Russian family, and against the backdrop of such grief the paternal and maternal sides of the family quarreled over the baby's burial: Would it be done according to Muslim or Christian ritual?

Of course, mixed marriages are extremely rare among practicing Muslims or Christians, but in situations where religion is a major part of identity even purely ritualistic elements can be sources of major conflict and misunderstanding. From the very beginning the question arises of whether to wed in a church or read a nikah. Some young families opt for both in order to keep their respective parents happy. "That is silly, because religious rituals become a game to keep parents at peace," Mukhametshin said.

Guzel Stolyarova has studied marriage and divorce records in Tatarstan spanning the past 50 years, and the share of mixed marriages did not decrease, even in the early 1990s when there was marked tension in Russian-Tatar relations in the republic and when the general number of marriages dropped by 50 percent due to economic difficulties and instability.

Today, she said, mixed marriages in Tatarstan constitute 25 to 30 percent of all marriages in the cities, and 15 to 18 percent in rural areas—one of the highest rates in Russia. Mukhametshin said such trends persist because the actual rate of people practicing their religion has remained low among both Russians and Tatars—about four percent.

This longing for traditional family roles and men who do not drink appears to be one of the factors that draw Russian women to marry Muslim men.

"There is no clear picture of whether poly-ethnic marriages are less stable," Stolyarova said. "I can say for sure that Tatar mono-ethnic marriages are stronger than Russian mono-ethnic marriages." But Stolyarova remains convinced that the ethnic factor is secondary when it comes to divorce.

Traditionalist Appeal

Ksenia D., a manager at a large media company in Moscow, is half-Russian and half-Adygei. Her parents divorced when she was a year old, and she said she does not know the details. But cultural differences, including her Adygei father's strong desire to have a son and not a daughter, were clearly part of the reason, she said. It was hard for her mother, a native of Moscow, to adapt to the Adygei lifestyle of her husband. As for Ksenia, although she grew up with her mother in Moscow, considers herself Christian, and only visits her father in the Adygeya Republic once in a while, she said that her Adygei roots mean a lot to her. "My father's tradition is dear to me, although I spend most of my life in Moscow," she said. The traditional family is very appealing to her. "The religious setting, the traditional roles in the family all make a lot of sense, and it is good to live in this clearly defined world," Ksenia said. "It is only natural for a man to be the breadwinner and protector and for the woman to bear children—far more natural than working 20 hours a day, as some of us do."

This longing for traditional family roles and men who do not drink appears to be one of the factors that draw Russian women to marry Muslim men. Korneva said it was important for her to realize that there is a religion that keeps people within a certain ethical framework. She said that prior to marrying her husband she studied literature about the role of women in Islam, and discovered that contrary to widely held stereotypes, it is a religion that is "very protective of women." "As for getting my permission to take a second wife, it is the subject of family jokes at the moment," she said.

A Cultural Alliance

Stolyarova said that the studies that she and her graduate students have conducted over the years, both in the archives of state record agencies and through polling people, have shown that conversion or a change in identity among spouses in Tatarstan is highly unlikely. "More likely, we observe an interaction where people adopt elements of the other culture—in the form of food, holidays, language. The dominant trend is cultural interaction," she said. "As far as children are concerned, it boils down to the eventual choice of ethnicity by the children. If in Soviet times the Russian side dominated, today we do not see that dominance. Many children choose a non-Russian identity—mainly Tatar. If parents are inclined to convey their culture to their children, they usually succeed. If it is not a priority for them, ethnicity becomes largely irrelevant for the children. They are children of the world—they nominally belong to some ethnicity, but practically cannot tell how it is different from the others."

One of these people with a mixed identity is 36-year-old Erkin Salakhetdinov, who works in Moscow at a research center affiliated with the Russian foreign ministry. His mother is originally from Leningrad, and his father took her to his Uzbek family in Kyrgyzstan. There, Salakhetdinov said, she had a hard time adapting to the life of a younger daughter-in-law in a local elite Soviet family, which was nonetheless fully based on Islamic traditions. "But she adapted, learned the language. We celebrated both the Islamic and Christian holidays—it was never a source of problems," he said. "I am a multicultural person. I can go into a mosque, church and synagogue. I believe that God is one. There is a saying that God gave people faith, and people invented religion in order to observe some canons."

When he was a child, his parents taught him that when asked which ethnicity he belongs to, the answer should be "a citizen of the Soviet Union." When the Soviet Union ceased to exist, he was forced to choose an identity and decided to be Uzbek. "But I speak English better than I speak Uzbek," he said. It is no wonder that he married a Russian. His younger sister chose to become a practicing Christian as a grown-up, and their father did not object.

Salakhetdinov is unabashedly positive about the globalist age in the area of intermarriage and ethnicity. "I have a friend whose mother is Russian and father is Kyrgyz. His wife is half-Jewish, half-German. Another friend is half-Tatar, half-Uzbek, and his wife is half-Russian, half-Georgian. What ethnicity are their children?" Salakhetdinov asked. "It is impossible to say which ethnic or religious environment they are growing up in. And imagine our grandchildren! It is a global trend. Look at the passionate propagandists of pure ethnicity—if not they themselves, then their children are likely to marry people of other ethnicities.

"Young people aged 16 to 20 do not mind ethnicity at all."

South Korea Does Not Support Multicultural Couples

Steven Borowiec

Steven Borowiec is a journalist. In the following viewpoint, he argues that the South Korean government needs to implement policies that support mixed couples and families, especially the thousands of foreign brides who marry South Korean men. Many of these women are victims of for-profit marriage brokers who do little to protect the brides or smooth the cultural transition for their clients. Another problem is that many mixed families live in poverty. According to Borowiec, South Korea must recognize its growing diversity and reject the idea that it is a uniform culture.

As you read, consider the following questions:

1. According to the Korea Institute for Health and Social Affairs, how many of the estimated 1.3 million foreigners residing in South Korea are foreign brides?

2. What percentage of foreign brides in South Korea are ethnic Koreans from China, according to a 2010 ministry for health survey?

3. According to government statistics, what percentage of mixed families live in near poverty?

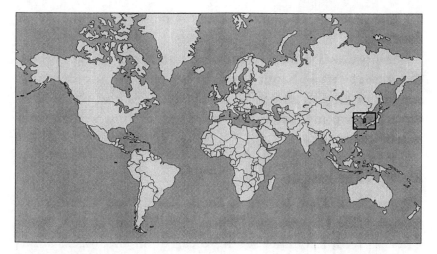

The murder would have been all the more horrifying had it been unprecedented.

On May 24 [2011], a South Korean man stabbed his Vietnamese wife to death while the couple's 19-day-old baby lay next to her. The man, a farmer, had been matched up with his foreign bride through a broker.

In 2010, another Vietnamese woman was killed by her husband a week after they were married. In 2008, a Vietnamese woman jumped from an apartment building to her death after being abused by her husband and mother-in-law.

These brutal acts highlight the ways ... in which South Korea is turning a blind eye to its rapidly changing demographics and the obstacles of integration.

A Growing Problem

For-profit marriage brokers operate without thorough oversight and the state agencies tasked with addressing the problem can't get their act together.

Or maybe they don't want to. South Korea is notoriously reluctant to accept migrants and change its identity as a homogenous culture.

The problem, of course, is that the migrants are already on their way.

South Korea is facing a growing number of foreign brides. On subway cars in South Korea, in between the ads for plastic surgery or English classes, brokerage agencies post wallet-sized cards that promise convenient marriages to kind women from nearby countries.

Many Challenges

Nguyen Ngoc Cam arrived in South Korea from Vietnam as a foreign bride 13 years ago. "It was very difficult at first. When I first arrived, I couldn't speak Korean at all and wasn't familiar with Korean culture," Nguyen, 35, said in a recent interview in Gwanghwamun Square, the symbolic epicenter of Seoul.

She said the government offered no help. "I was left to rely on myself. The important thing was that I developed confidence over time."

Ultimately, Nguyen adapted to life in Namyangju, a suburb east of Seoul, and learned to speak to her husband, a construction engineer. The couple has two children, ages 10 and 12.

On subway cars in South Korea, in between the ads for plastic surgery or English classes, brokerage agencies post wallet-sized cards that promise convenient marriages to kind women from nearby countries.

Foreign Brides

More than 100,000 of the estimated 1.2 million foreigners residing in South Korea are foreign brides, according to the Korea Institute for Health and Social Affairs.

Vietnamese and Filipino women make up 19.5 and 6.6 percent of that population, respectively, according to a March

For-Profit Marriages in South Korea

Koreans . . . spend an average of 13 million won ($10,600) in costs for interracial marriages, according to the Korea Consumer Agency (KCA). There are 1,044 matchmaking companies in Korea. The most popular country as the source of "brides" was Vietnam following China. It takes an average of 88 days, or about three months, to complete an interracial marriage through agencies—from the Korean applicant's departure to interview with his prospective spouse and their entry to Korea. Global mixed marriages have a gender and social equity dimension: The male is from a rich country, and the female is from a poor country.

Maragtas S.V. Amante,
"Korea—Pinoy Mixed Marriages and Tensions
in the Multicultural Family," ABS-CBNnews.com,
November 22, 2009.

2010 survey by the ministry for health. Ethnic Koreans from China make up the largest portion at 30.4 percent, with Han Chinese at 27.3 percent.

A Lack of Government Assistance

But besides keeping a tally, government agencies have yet to make a significant impact in smoothing the transition. A lack of coordination among the three ministries—gender, education and health—responsible for assisting multiethnic families means it's hard to get anything done. (Case in point: None of the three ministries returned requests for comment for this [viewpoint].)

Brokers do little to prepare the brides. Language and cultural issues aside, both men charged with murdering their

Vietnamese wives had known histories of mental health issues that weren't disclosed to their brides in advance.

At a memorial service outside the South Korean Ministry of Gender Equality [and Family] on June 2, protesters carried placards that read "Brokers: do you see what you have done?" But it isn't only the wives who suffer. Mixed families struggle economically and multiethnic children don't fare as well academically as fully Korean kids.

Mixed Families in South Korea

Nearly 60 percent of multicultural families in a government survey were living in near poverty, with a household income of less than 2 million won ($1,850) per month. Average household income in South Korea is 3.3 million won ($3,065) per month.

Also according to government stats, 80.8 percent of the children from multiethnic families aged 7 to 12 go to school. But only 26.5 percent make it to high school—far below average in a country that has one of the most educated societies in the world.

Kim Hee-kyung, director of advocacy for Save the Children Korea, argues that it isn't just newcomers that need help assimilating, but it is also full Koreans who need to learn how to welcome different cultures.

Mixed families struggle economically and multiethnic children don't fare as well academically as fully Korean kids.

"We keep urging the government to focus more on the education of fully Korean children," said Kim.

"It is time to educate the majority of children, not just the minority. But the government's policy focuses only on how to integrate this minority into Korean society; they don't accept diversity."

A Uniform Culture

The crux of the problem is that South Korean society resists thinking of itself as anything other than a uniform culture.

"We need to discard the centuries-old concept of Korea as a homogeneous, monocultural sort of society and accept that we are becoming more diverse," said Lee Chan-boum of the Presidential Council on Nation Branding, a government body that promotes South Korea's image internationally.

Koreans commonly believe, and are taught in school, that their people have populated the peninsula from time immemorial and have withstood colonial occupation and other forms of outside interference with their uniquely pure culture intact.

Brian [Reynolds "B.R."] Myers, director of international studies at Dongseo University in Busan, argues in his work, *The Cleanest Race*, that it wasn't until the arrival of the Japanese in the late 19th century that a uniquely Korean identity began to be formed in both emulation of and opposition to the colonial presence. Contact with Chinese and Japanese invaders created a mixed bloodline.

At present, there are no government programs to educate full South Koreans on accepting different cultures, which Kim of Save the Children says is the logical next step.

"Usually mixed children don't recognize that they're different; they are categorized as being different. The government only urges children to learn Korean, not Vietnamese. Through this, the children start to think that Vietnamese is inferior to Korean," Kim said. "They then start to hate everything from Vietnam."

Periodical and Internet Sources Bibliography

The following articles have been selected to supplement the diverse views presented in this chapter.

Abiodun Awolaja	"Inter-tribal Marriage: What Pain, What Gain?," *Nigerian Tribune*, December 20, 2010.
Zara Badawi	"Mixed Race Marriage: 'My Race Didn't Fit,'" *Independent* (United Kingdom), July 17, 2012.
Alexia Cahyaningtyas	"Watatita: The Hardships of Mixed Marriage Couples," *Jakarta Globe*, June 18, 2012.
G. Elijah Dann	"Kentucky Fried Bible Reading: Is Interracial Marriage Immoral?," *Huffington Post*, December 2, 2011.
Katie Engelhart	"In Bosnia, Divided They Stall," *Maclean's*, December 20, 2011.
Katherine Feeney	"When Cultures Clash," *Sydney Morning Herald*, September 5, 2012.
Kevin Noble Maillard	"Do Barriers to Interracial Marriage Still Exist?," The Grio, May 1, 2012.
Elizabeth Namazzi	"Marrying from the 'Wrong' Tribe," *New Vision* (Uganda), March 24, 2007.
Pathik Pathak	"Cross-Cultural Marriage Is No Picnic," *Guardian*, January 11, 2010.
Rong Xiaoqing	"Dissonant Wedding Bells: Generations Clash over Asian Mixed Marriages," New America Media, April 29, 2011.
Slavoj Zizek	"Israel's Best Hope Lies in a Single State," *New Statesman*, March 4, 2011.

GLOBALVIEWPOINTS

CHAPTER

Some Consequences of Mixed Marriage

The Global Prevalence of Interracial Marriage Will Eventually Blur Racial Distinctions

Matthew Syed

Matthew Syed is a British journalist and broadcaster. In the following viewpoint, he finds that the growing global trend of interracial marriage functions to connect different races and obscure racial distinctions. Syed points out that recent scientific discoveries, particularly the Human Genome Project, prove that there is little genetic variation between population groups. Racial categories, as they are perceived, are superficial—but humans continue to classify people because it is a natural reaction to unfamiliarity. Syed argues that mixed-race children break down such classifications and challenge people's perception of racial differences.

As you read, consider the following questions:

1. According to the author, how many US states had anti-miscegenation laws in the 1960s?
2. What does the author report is the rarest kind of interracial marriage in the United States?

3. How long ago does the author say that our ancestors migrated from Africa to populate the rest of the world?

When my parents tied the knot in the mid-sixties their respective families were more than a little shocked. My dad is a dark-skinned Pakistani who came to England to study, my mum an auburn-haired, freckled lass from the Welsh valleys. Few of the prospective in-laws approved of the marriage, although both sides of the family were eventually reconciled to the idea, particularly when my parents started having supercute children (their second son was, apparently, particularly cuddly). In the meantime, my parents faced an uphill and rather daunting struggle for social acceptability.

Miscegenation

In many ways, they were the lucky ones. If interracial couples in sixties Britain faced everything from ghoulish curiosity to downright hostility, American couples faced a period in the slammer. Marrying across the racial divide went by the ugly term "miscegenation" and was a criminal offence in 16 states including Florida, Texas and Oklahoma. Southern attitudes were perhaps best summed up by a judge passing sentence on a mixed-race couple in 1961: "Almighty God created the races white, black, yellow, Malay and red, and he placed them on several continents. But for the interference with his arrangement there would be no cause for such marriages." They were ordered to leave the state for 25 years or face 12 months in prison.

Such sentiments were not the exclusive preserve of rednecks: They existed among northern liberals, too, something satirised marvelously in the 1967 classic *Guess Who's Coming to Dinner*, in which a black doctor, played by Sidney Poitier, gets engaged to a white student whom he meets on holiday. The many ironies of racial identity are captured in an unforgettable sequence when Poitier meets the parents (spellbindingly played by Spencer Tracy and Katharine

Hepburn) who, despite impeccable liberal credentials, are visibly shocked when they come face to face with their prospective son-in-law. "Mom," the daughter says in surprise, "he thinks you are going to faint because he is a Negro!"

Mixed-Race Kids

But if the atavistic reactions and social paradoxes of the sixties and seventies seem like ancient history, it is worth remembering that they formed the backdrop of daily existence for the sprinkling of mixed-race kids who grew up in that transformative era: Barack Obama was born to a Kenyan father and white mother in Hawaii in 1961, and spent much of his childhood in racially divided America, albeit in ethnically mixed Hawaii. Paul Boateng, the former British cabinet minister, was born to a Ghanaian father and Scottish mother. A new generation of mixed-racers include Tiger Woods (mixed-race father and mother), Lewis Hamilton (Afro-Caribbean father and white mother), Zadie Smith (English father and Jamaican mother) and Malcolm Gladwell (English father and Jamaican-born mother).

In almost every measure of social progress, mixed-race kids fare somewhere between whites and blacks (blacks, incidentally, continue to fare significantly worse than whites in everything from income to life expectancy), but there is one area where they shoot off the scale—risk taking. It does not take a huge leap of imagination to understand why.

As Roland Fryer, a Harvard economist, puts it: "Mixed race adolescents—not having a natural peer group—need to engage in risky behaviour to be accepted." This is not to imply that all mixed-race teenagers are afflicted by a sense of divided identity, but merely that, at a population level, there are measurable and often dramatic consequences—which may explain the emergence of mixed-race highflyers. Although interracial marriages are more common today than in the sixties, they remain surprisingly rare, particularly in the United States

"Mum...Dad... you don't know what it's like for me, being mixed race."

where just 1 per cent of white marriages and 5 per cent of black marriages are across the racial divide. The rarest kind of interracial marriage is between white men and black women; the most common is between white men and Asian women. In the UK [United Kingdom] things are moving faster, largely because communities are much less ghettoised.

Globalisation and Race

According to a report by the Equality and Human Rights Commission, published yesterday [January 19, 2009], half of men and a third of women with Caribbean heritage who are in couples are with partners of a different race. But this drops to well under 10 per cent of Bangladeshi men and women.

While racial mixing is increasing only gradually in global terms, the trend has provoked some dramatic predictions. In a speech last year, Steve Jones, professor of genetics at University College London, argued that we will soon witness the complete obliteration of the races: "Worldwide, all populations are becoming connected," he said. "History is made in bed, but nowadays the beds are getting closer together. We are mixing into a global mass, and the future is brown."

This is one of the less talked-about consequences of globalisation and is the outcome that anti-miscegenation laws (finally struck down by the US Supreme Court in 1967) were designed to avoid. Although this vision is still a long way off, it is worth asking how you feel about the prospect of a mongrelised human future: Does it fill you with horror or excitement (or possibly both)?

While racial mixing is increasing only gradually in global terms, the trend has provoked some dramatic predictions.

Race and Identity

Before answering this question, try this one instead: What is race? In the census data, it is defined by self-identity: You are given a choice of boxes to tick—mixed race became a category in the UK only in the last census of 2001—and the statisticians take it from there. You might suppose that this is a time-saving device and that a clever scientist could give you a definitive classification with a blood test or a mouth swab, but you would be wrong. One of the most striking things to emerge from the Human Genome Project is that the human species is, genetically speaking, remarkably uniform and that the little genetic variation that exists is found within population groups (about 90 per cent) as opposed to between population groups (around 10 per cent). The categories that we call races blend seamlessly into each other and have no genetically defined boundaries.

Why? Because, until very recently, all humans lived together in Africa (yes, we all have African roots). The migration of our ancestors into the rest of the world probably happened only within the past 70,000 years, so natural selection has had very little time to get to work on driving the continental groups apart. The differences that do exist, such as skin colour and nose shape, are, genetically speaking, superficial.

As Henry Harpending, the American geneticist, put it, humans are a bit like PCs: "Computers are divisible into major races—Compaq, Dell, Gateway, Micron—as well as many minor populations. These computer races are like human races. Are there deep essential differences? Hardly. Take the cases off and we can barely tell them apart. The components of PCs are commodities that are completely interchangeable. Human race differences are like that." In other words, the differences between the races are many times greater if we look at the label than if we look inside. That is not to say that there are no genetic differences at all, but that they are small on-average differences. When meeting someone new, it makes sense to judge them on their abilities rather than their label.

Race and Psychology

But this is easier said than done. The problem is that we make "label judgments" and it is this, I think, that helps to explain why gaping divisions continue to exist between the races on everything from income levels to marital intimacy, and why mixed-race kids feel the need to take big risks to be accepted. If you think, that you are immune to such judgments it might be worth checking out the Harvard Implicit Association Test website: You might be surprised—rather as Spencer Tracy and Katharine Hepburn were in *Guess Who's Coming to Dinner*—at what your subconscious is really like. I rated as having a "strong automatic preference for European Americans compared to African Americans", since you ask.

This is not a case of bigotry but of psychology. Our brains, seeking to make sense of the complexity of the world, instinctively divide things into categories to speed up processing. It makes computational sense to make crude generalisations about minority groups—this is why we find it more difficult, for example, to discern facial differences in other races that are perfectly obvious within our own ("they all look the same to me"). But these biases break down with familiarity. One study showed that something as trivial as watching basketball (which has many African American players) caused whites to be much better at recognising black faces.

This is why mixed-race kids should not be seen as evidence of a looming racial apocalypse but as the reproductive consequences of a rather uplifting kind of barrier breaking. According to Ludi Simpson, professor of population studies at Manchester University, integration tends to have a beneficial impact on the prevalence of racism. "Local surveys indicate that most people regard racial integration as benign when it happens in their own backyard. It is only when they are asked about racial integration more generally that the responses tend to be negative, largely because the media tends to exaggerate the issue."

The barriers between human population groups never had much basis in genetics, but were constructed from feelings of unfamiliarity. In this sense, the likes of Obama, Hamilton and Woods are the poster boys for a new and exciting type of globalisation. We usually look to governments to solve the problems of the world; in this case, we should also look to bedrooms.

Mixed Race Doesn't Mean "Fitter"

In some quarters, there is a belief that mixed-race individuals are genetically "fitter" than those born to parents of the same race. Being fitter in this sense means that you have a head start in the reproductive stakes because you are more beautiful (and so find a mate more easily) and/or because you are healthier (and thus will have children more likely to survive to breeding age).

This "hybrid vigour" argument—the term is usually applied to plants—can be thought of as the polar opposite to inbreeding. If inbreeding is bad, then the blending of two dramatically different gene pools must, the theory goes, lead to genetic nirvana. Such theories are hinted at in comments about the attractiveness of mixed-race people; they were espoused more fully in Alon Ziv's controversial book *Breeding Between the Lines: Why Interracial People Are Healthier and More Attractive*.

The barriers between human population groups never had much basis in genetics, but were constructed from feelings of unfamiliarity.

And they are seemingly confirmed by the success of "mutts" such as Barack Obama, Tiger Woods and Lewis Hamilton.

The theory, however, does not stand up to real scrutiny. Inbreeding does indeed bring problems; infants born to first-cousin marriages have a higher than average rate of congenital heart problems. In Britain, children of Pakistani origin are disproportionately affected by certain genetic disorders, thought to arise from the culture of consanguineous marriages (between close relatives). On the other hand, health studies also show that there are no startling benefits accruing to children of mixed parentage.

Overall, the rate of birth defects among mixed-race babies seems to be the same as for other babies, reinforcing the idea that, while people might come in different coloured envelopes, the contents are not that genetically distinct.

Turks with African Ancestors Want Their Existence to Be Felt

Ayşe Karabat

Ayşe Karabat is a contributor to Today's Zaman. *In the following viewpoint, she discusses the challenges faced by the Afro-Turk community in Turkey. Throughout the years, many Afro-Turks, descendants of African citizens of the Ottoman Empire, have intermarried with native Turks, and the children of these mixed unions often face prejudice and misconceptions. Many must deal with superstitious beliefs about Africans. A welcome sign is that a traditional festival known as Dana Bayrami is being revived, and Afro-Turk culture is being recognized by the larger society.*

As you read, consider the following questions:

1. According to the author, where do the majority of Afro-Turks live?
2. What is the Treaty of Lausanne?
3. What does the author say that Afro-Turks are called in Turkey?

While preparing a barbecue in the crowded picnic area of Izmir's Eşrefpaşa district, they sing old Turkish pop songs and eat Turkey's indispensable picnic food: stuffed grape leaves cooked with olive oil.

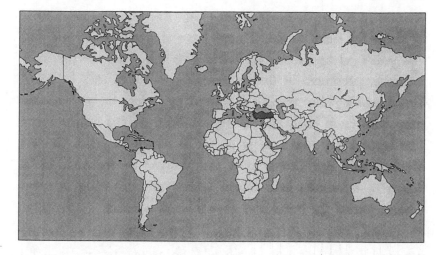

As in any typical Turkish family, the men are preparing the "mangal" barbecue while talking about soccer matches or recent political developments. The heroic acts of their grandparents in the War of Independence also feature prominently in discussions. The old women chat with one another and wear head scarves, as do most older women in Turkey.

Who are these people? Mehmet, Ali, Ayşe, Rabia, Arzu, Emine, Hatice and Hüseyin, to name a few. Everything is typically Turkish except for one detail: They are black. Afro-Turks, as they prefer to be called, are the descendants of African citizens of the Ottoman Empire. They have come together under the African Solidarity and Cooperation Association (ASCA) to revitalize one of their oldest traditions—a holiday celebrated by their grandparents: Dana Bayrami, or the Calf Festival.

Deniz Yükseker, a professor in Koç University's department of sociology, gave a speech on the culture of Afro-Turks during a conference held at Ege University. Dana Bayrami was celebrated from 1880 until the end of the 1920s. "Leaders of the Afro-Turk community, known as 'godya,' used to collect money in order to buy a cow. On the first Saturday of each May, they sacrificed this cow. Failing to make this sacrifice would cause draughts, according to popular folklore," Yükseker explains.

She adds that in those years, Dana Bayrami was celebrated in Izmir for three weeks. Things have changed over time and this year's celebrations only lasted two days. On the first day, Yükseker presented at the conference on the history of Afro-Turks, and a photo exhibit prepared by Özlem Sümer showed snapshots from daily life as experienced by the community. The second day saw a large picnic at which Boğaziçi Gösteri Merkezi and Ege University's music band performed. Melis Sökmen, a famous jazz singer whose grandmother is from Ghana, joined the band and gave a small concert.

During this year's Dana Bayrami, the focus was on having fun and a cow was not sacrificed. "Some of our friends said that it would be fine to sacrifice a sheep, but maybe next year," says ASCA chairman Mustafa Olpak. He points out that Dana Bayrami used to be an opportunity for their ancestors to have a family reunion. The festival served as a venue at which members of a family dispersed by slavery would come together.

Afro-Turks, as they prefer to be called, are the descendants of African citizens of the Ottoman Empire.

Gülay Kayacan, who works for the History Foundation, an institute that researches and publishes articles on Turkish history, says that some of the Afro-Turks are descendants of slaves who used to work on farms or in houses. Slaves working in agriculture were concentrated in areas where cotton production was high. It is for this reason that most Afro-Turks today live on the Aegean coast and some in the Mediterranean region.

"Some 10,000 slaves, black and white, were brought into the Ottoman Empire every year. During the constitutional monarchy period (1876–1878), slavery was abolished and former slaves settled in areas where they used to work. Some of them were even given land by the government," Kayacan says.

Kayacan is the coordinator of the History Foundation's "Voices Coming from a Silent Past" project, supported by the European Union Commission Delegation in Turkey. She underlines that their oral history project aims to form an archive that will aid in researching the cultural, economic and social status of Afro-Turks today and to place them in the mosaic of history. To this end, the foundation is recording the personal histories of the Afro-Turk community.

"Unfortunately, most of the elders of the Afro-Turk community who could remember the stories of immigration and the cultural aspects of the community have passed away. Written documentation is also scarce, so we are trying to preserve this undocumented past before it is too late," Kayacan says. According to personal accounts collected so far, the ancestors of Afro-Turks came from various countries, including present-day Niger, Egypt, Saudi Arabia, Libya, Kenya and Sudan. In fact, the Embassy of Sudan sent a representative to participate in this year's Dana Bayrami.

Kayacan also notes that some of the descendants of former slaves remain poor. Educational opportunities for them have been scarce and they are generally not property owners. The number of Afro-Turks graduating from universities is below the national average and most women tend to be agricultural workers if they live in villages or housewives if they live in the urban areas. The women that have found opportunities to become educated work as midwives or nurses.

Not all of the Afro-Turks' ancestors were slaves. Some came from the island of Crete following the Lausanne Treaty, signed in 1924. This treaty called for a population exchange between the Greek Orthodox citizens of the young Turkish republic and the Muslim citizens of Greece. Most of the blacks on Crete were Muslims, so they were subjected to this popula-

Interesting Facts About Izmir

- Izmir was established at least 5000 years ago

- Epic poet Homer (9th century BC), the author of *The Iliad* and *The Odyssey*, was born in Izmir

- Three of the "Seven Churches" which were mentioned in the Book of Revelation [in the Bible] are in Izmir

- Parchment paper was first invented in Pergamon, in the district of Izmir

- The Phokaians, ancient residents of the city, built 50-oared boats carrying 500 passengers

"Izmir, Turkey: Interesting Facts About Izmir,"
TurkeyCentral.com, 2012.

tion exchange. Like many others who were moved through this population exchange, they settled on the Aegean coast, mainly around Izmir. Eighty-year-old Emine Konaçer's mother and Olpak's family were among these immigrants.

Konaçer's mother spoke only Greek, which explains why Konaçer is bilingual. She and her husband have four children, including Mehmet Konaçer (48), a physical education teacher.

"When I was young, our neighbors would sometimes speak in Greek on our street in Ayvalik and I used to shout at them: 'Citizen, speak Turkish!'" he says. At the time, the Turkish government had launched a program calling on all citizens to speak only Turkish.

Mehmet Konaçer enjoys dancing the traditional folklore dances of the Aegean area and he performed a dance for the crowd at this year's Dana Bayrami.

As with every teacher, his students coin nicknames for him. "They first used to call me Clay [after the famous African American boxer Cassius Clay, later known as Muhammad Ali]. But nicknames come and go. As other blacks become famous, the nickname my students choose for me changes," he says.

Konaçer is married and has two children. As is the case with multiracial children, they take on the features of both parents. This is the case with many Afro-Turks as the small community has many interracial marriages. Some Afro-Turks are blond and some have green eyes, like Konaçer's cousin, Hüseyin Hançer.

Being "different" has, however, also led to discrimination. The society at large holds many misconceptions about Afro-Turks.

"Our interviews show that Afro-Turks living in villages do not feel discriminated against. They are not labeled as the 'other' or excluded. In a village, everyone has known one another since birth. Cities, on the other hand, are a different matter altogether, though Anatolia is still a land that is able to absorb a variety of cultures," Kayacan says.

Ayşe Sözer, a young Afro-Turk, says that Turkish society does not have a racist approach, but that sometimes the Afro-Turk community does experience "exaggerated interest" and social discrimination from society.

"I am asked many odd questions; for example, some ask if I get whiter by taking baths. Sometimes people stare at me and end up tripping or bumping into a pole. I have learned to not get angry at people, but when I was at the university, my roommate left our dorm room because she said she was afraid to live with someone that is black," Sözer says.

Sometimes people have a hard time believing that Afro-Turks are Turks. On one occasion, Sözer was shopping in Denizli and the shopkeeper, mistaking her for a tourist speaking in perfect Turkish, tried to compliment her by saying she speaks Turkish better than him, a native Turk.

Not being considered a "Turk" can at times be problematic. Most Afro-Turks live in the Aegean region, famous for human smuggling. This has cast suspicion on the Afro-Turk community.

Locals in the Aegean region also have some superstitious beliefs about "black people." Some believe that if they see a black person and pinch the person next to them, their wishes will come true. Sözer recalled one case in which two ladies pinched each other upon seeing her. She was understandably upset. "I told the ladies that if they really wanted their wishes to come true, I also had to pinch both of them! They accepted and I pinched them very hard," she says, laughing.

Sometimes people have a hard time believing that Afro-Turks are Turks.

Another superstition some hold is that the kiss of a black person can bring luck. "When I was small, I was asked to kiss many girls because there was this superstition that if a girl does not get kissed by a small African child, she would not find a husband," Olpak says.

Apart from being the focus of some superstitions, most Afro-Turks say they have never been humiliated or discriminated against by the society. However, overcoming prejudice while looking for someone to marry is not as easy as one would hope. Kayacan notes that sometimes the family does not approve of their son or daughter marrying an Afro-Turk.

Afro-Turks are often called "Arabs" in Turkey. They also refer to themselves as Arabs, at times. This has led to a situation in which "Arab" means "black." Ege University professor Ahmet Yürür explains. "For the Turks, Africa was only the northern part of the continent: from Egypt to Morocco. This part was of course under Arab influence. Turks were never really interested in the south of the continent. This is why this community has come to be called 'Arab,'" he says.

Yürür suggests that Turkey can build bridges between itself and Africa with the help of Afro-Turks. But even establishing an association was difficult, Olpak says.

"Our people did not even know of the word 'association.' They were suspicious at first, but in Turkey, all ethnic groups have solidarity associations except for us. We had some difficulties at first because we lived in a closed society," he says. This is not to say that Olpak is pessimistic. Dana Bayrami is evidence that the Afro-Turk community is being revived.

Olpak has authored two books: *Slave Woman Kemale*, which tells the story of his own family, a slave family from Kenya that lived on Crete and had to migrate to Turkey, and *The Shores of Slaves*, in which Olpak presents a collection of stories by other Afro-Turks.

"I am a third generation Afro-Turk. My grandparents were slaves. The first generation lived through the sad events, the second generation tried to forget and deny these events, but the third generation wants to know what happened and how," Olpak says, adding: "We are black and we are from here. We are a part of this rich Anatolian culture and we are ready to make an effort to be noticed by the society. I believe that in this way we will be able to contribute to the tolerant culture of this beautiful land." Olpak has a wish for his community: to celebrate Dana Bayrami on the national level one day as a festival of tolerance.

Rising Mixed Marriages Set New Societal Trend

Lisa Conrad

Lisa Conrad is a reporter for the Kuwait Times. *In the following viewpoint, she investigates a growing trend of Kuwaiti men marrying foreign women. Statistics show that these mixed marriages have lower divorce rates than marriages between Kuwaiti citizens. Conrad reports that mixed marriages last longer because they are not arranged marriages and are built on solid foundations. Conrad argues that marrying outside the Kuwaiti culture may be attractive for some men who have bad reputations or want to escape the strict social, familial, and financial commitments that come with marriage to a Kuwaiti women.*

As you read, consider the following questions:

1. According to a report by a local Arabic daily, what is the divorce rate for Kuwaiti couples?

2. According to the same report, what is the divorce rate of mixed marriages in Kuwait?

3. What do some Kuwaiti men cite as some of the financial considerations of marrying a Kuwaiti woman?

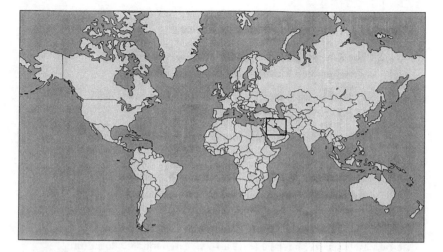

The instance of Kuwaiti men marrying foreign women has been rising steadily in recent years. According to a report by a local Arabic daily, it is fuelling fears that the numbers of unmarried Kuwaiti women will increase as a result. What's more, the report found that the instance of divorce is much lower between a Kuwaiti and a non-Kuwaiti than between two Kuwaitis. The daily reported that an entire committee was formed to try and curb the trend, which they failed to manage. The trends, and the committee, have received much attention but the question remains as to why it's becoming more common, and why resulting marriages are more likely to prevail. According to the report, the differences are astounding: 63 percent of Kuwaiti couples ended up divorcing, whereas mixed marriages enjoyed a miniscule 13 percent divorce rate.

According to 27-year-old Bader, mixed marriages last longer not because of nationality, but because they're built on more solid foundations, "I don't think that nationality is the determining factor in divorce rates. Usually marriages are arranged and families seek spouses within their circle of acquaintances and distant or close relatives. So, the marriage between two complete strangers results in a lot of misunderstandings and end in divorce." He added, "Because, tradition-

---

Mixed Marriage and Divorce in Kuwait

- For Kuwait, the big majority of all mixed marriages were between Kuwaitis and Arab nationals.

- 77% of Kuwaiti men married to non-Kuwaiti women (Arabs).

- 78% of Kuwaiti women married to non-Kuwaiti men (Arabs).

- Divorce rate in 2004: 45% for Kuwaiti men and 77% for Kuwaiti women married to non-nationals.

TAKEN FROM: Layachi Anser, "Divorce in Gulf Societies: A Major Challenge to Marriage and Family," The Doha Colloquium: Strengthening Marriage and Supporting Families, October 6–7, 2009.

---

ally, mothers don't seek foreigner brides or grooms for their kids, one can say that almost all marriages between Kuwaitis and non-Kuwaitis are not arranged. The couples here have met outside the circle of the family. They are not complete strangers to one another."

Hanaa, a 22-year-old, agreed, "There are a lot more foreigners in Kuwait now and there's not as much pressure as there was before about marrying a Kuwaiti, so nationality isn't as much of a focus."

While Hanaa and Bader feel that the trend is linked to circumstance and globalization, others insist that it is based not on nationality, but on culture. "Do you know how much it costs to marry a Kuwaiti woman?" asked 25-year-old Abdulrahman. "The amount of gifts you have to give and the dowry and the house; it's a huge sum. Plus, it's still not the norm with Kuwaiti women to contribute to the household, and not all Kuwaiti women work. So you can expect high financial costs for good, especially since they like, and will often demand, the finer things in life."

For Adbulrahman, the issue of finance is a serious one that he intends to keep in mind when choosing a partner, "These cultural customs will cost you a lot in the long term. I'm happy to pamper my wife, but there are limits. I wouldn't mind the customs if they were more of a choice and less influential. At the end of the day, if you marry a foreigner, especially a Western woman, you're looking at more balance in your marriage. Plus, when you marry a foreigner you don't have the same pressures regarding family name and family background. If you marry a Kuwaiti, you do, so it can be more limiting."

There is no single, concrete reason behind the rising trend of mixed marriages and their increased likelihood of long-term success.

Power of Reputation

Fida, a Lebanese expatriate engaged to a Kuwaiti, agreed that culture is a central issue, "Kuwaiti society is very close and interlinked, and marrying within it deepens your connection to it even further. If you marry a non-Kuwaiti, the consequences of divorce aren't so deeply tied into all of your social and family circles in the same way they are if you marry a Kuwaiti." She added, "With Kuwaiti women, and most Arab women, you have to ask for her hand in marriage from her father. The difference here though is that reputation means so much and men can be rejected if they don't meet certain standards. For example a friend of mine was rejected for having a reputation for travelling to Bahrain and Dubai to go clubbing with friends."

The power of reputation is evident in this example as Fida continued, "After that, he gave up on the idea of marrying a Kuwaiti woman. His reputation was tarnished and he knew the women he would consider would reject him. With foreigners, especially Westerners, you don't have to prove yourself to anyone but her." In addition to lesser social pressures, Fida added that the children born of a Kuwaiti father and a non-Kuwaiti mother will still enjoy full rights, full nationality and all the benefits that come along with it.

There is no single, concrete reason behind the rising trend of mixed marriages and their increased likelihood of long-term success. Unless, of course, you ask 32-year-old Maha, "If men have the chance to be lazy, they will. Kuwaiti men love the idea of traditional women, and many of us still respect those values even if we have a career as well. But they also love the idea of reducing their responsibilities, and that wins out with some of them." She added, "Some arranged marriages fail, and some mixed marriages are because of love. But this trend, I think, is because Kuwaiti men no longer want to commit to their traditional responsibilities and, to be honest, we don't want the ones who don't anyway."

The United Arab Emirates Benefits from Mixed Marriages

Sultan Al Qassemi

Sultan Al Qassemi is a journalist and fellow at the Dubai School of Government. In the following viewpoint, he responds to recent controversial comments made by the Grand Mufti of Dubai, Dr. Ahmed Al Haddad, who questioned whether there should be restrictions on citizens of the United Arab Emirates marrying foreigners. Also, he questioned the loyalty of Emiratis who are born to a foreign parent. Qassemi states that such questions are unfair, un-Islamic, and un-Emirati. Qassemi further argues that the United Arab Emirates should be more welcoming and should appreciate the contributions of Emiratis born to mixed marriages.

As you read, consider the following questions:

1. What does the author say that Ali Mostafa does?

2. Who does the author identify as "one of the principal architects behind the Abu Dhabi 2030 Economic Vision"?

3. What recommendations did the author make to build civic participation for Emiratis?

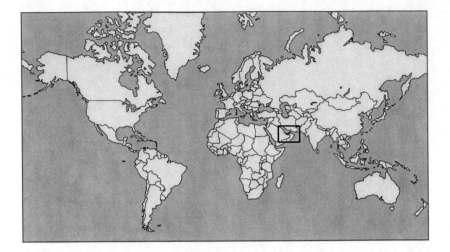

Not too long ago, I boarded a plane in Dubai bound for the United States. There were a number of Emirati [citizens of the United Arab Emirates] families on board, some of whom I recognised and greeted. After a 14-hour direct flight, we descended from the plane and made our way to passport control. One Emirati family walked towards the line for US citizens and, in my naivety, I almost told them they were standing in the wrong queue. I hesitated, correctly it turned out. They were American citizens and obliged to stand in the US citizens section.

A Firestorm

Many people who hear this story immediately assume that the mother was a foreigner. Not only is that incorrect—the mother a true-blue Emirati—but she also works in the UAE [United Arab Emirates] government. In the past week [in August 2010], I was reminded of this by an article in the *National* relating to mixed parentage. The Grand Mufti of Dubai, Dr Ahmed Al Haddad, made controversial comments questioning whether there should be restrictions on Emiratis marrying outside their nationality.

In truth, a substantial number of talented Emiratis have been born to mixed marriages, a point that Dr Al Haddad's comments did not seem to take into consideration. According to one person who was present at the panel discussion, Emiratis from mixed marriages may have "mixed loyalties". So are they Emirati enough? Well, let us take a look at some of these Emiratis to find out. Ali Mostafa, the director behind *City of Life*, is the product of a mixed marriage. *City of Life*, which depicts contemporary life in Dubai in a powerful and realistic fashion, has become an international ambassador for the UAE after opening in Australia and Canada with a screening scheduled in Washington, DC. Is its director Emirati enough?

Omar Saif Ghobash and Yousef Al Otaiba, the UAE ambassadors to Russia and the United States respectively, both have foreign-born mothers and yet they serve the UAE with as much attention and dedication as any other Emirati ambassador. I have written before about how Mr Al Otaiba has worked tirelessly on behalf of the country, in particular on the nuclear 123 agreement with the United States. Mr Ghobash speaks six languages and was heavily involved in bringing New York University to the UAE's capital. Are they Emirati enough?

More Examples of Prominent Emiratis

Razan Al Mubarak is also a product of a mixed marriage. Her late father, like Ambassador Ghobash's, gave his life for the country. Ms Al Mubarak, in her roles as assistant secretary general of the Environment Agency–Abu Dhabi and managing director of the Emirates Wildlife Society, is busy protecting the country's wildlife on both land and sea. Is she Emirati enough? At Abu Dhabi's strategic investment arm Mubadala, the chief operations officer, Waleed Al Mokarrab Al Muhairi, also happens to be chairman of Yahsat [Al Yah Satellite Communications Company], Advanced Technology Investment Company and Cleveland Clinic Abu Dhabi. But perhaps most importantly, he is credited with being "one of the principal architects behind the Abu Dhabi 2030 Economic Vision". And yes, Mr al Mokarrab comes from a mixed family.

The truth is the UAE is a richer country because of these individuals of mixed backgrounds.

Wael Al-Sayegh is a writer, poet, translator and founder of the consultancy firm Al-Ghaf, which delivers "inter-cultural induction programmes to multinational organisations serving the region". Mr Al-Sayegh has spoken to many multinational corporations about UAE culture and offered a Dubai perspective to foreign news outlets, including the BBC, during recent high-profile criminal cases. Is he Emirati enough?

Sarah Shaw, an Emirati whose biological father is English, currently works at the General Secretariat of the Abu Dhabi Executive Council and is a huge supporter of Emiratisation. Is she Emirati enough? Other Emiratis from mixed families who have made substantial contributions include the director general of the Dubai World Trade Centre, Helal Saeed Al Marri, the film director Nawaf Al-Janahi and the columnist Mishaal Al Gergawi, among many others.

There are examples in my immediate circle of Emirati friends who genuinely care about this country, not despite one of their parents being foreign born but perhaps because of it. Should the UAE, and specifically Dubai, known for being hospitable and welcoming to people of all ethnicities, backgrounds and cultures, make our very own citizens feel unwelcome? The truth is the UAE is a richer country because of these individuals of mixed backgrounds. What we should concentrate on is strengthening the ties that people have to this great nation. I have previously suggested military service for Emirati high school graduates, cultural immersion and social volunteering as ways to build civic participation.

Frankly, it would be insulting to question the loyalty of Emiratis who are born to a foreign parent. It is also unfair, un-Islamic and ultimately in this case un-Emirati to generalise about people of any background. The Emirates is a vibrant country of many colours—only seeing a single shade excludes too many of its strengths.

Mixed Couples in Croatia and Bosnia and Herzegovina Face Ethnic Intolerance and Discrimination

Barbara Matejcic

Barbara Matejcic is a Croatian journalist. In the following viewpoint, she reports that mixed couples in Croatia and Bosnia and Herzegovina, particularly in the historically ethnically diverse cities of Mostar and Vukovar, are stigmatized and often face ethnic intimidation and intolerance. As a result of the devastating wars of the 1990s that were spurred by stoking nationalistic and ethnic tensions, communities that were once multicultural and tolerant have been ripped apart by prejudice and hate. Matejcic says the situation is slow to change because ethnic groups have segregated themselves into enclaves, and there is little ethnic mixing, especially in schools. She finds that many mixed couples migrate to more tolerant countries to raise their children away from the ethnic tension.

As you read, consider the following questions:

1. What does the author identify as the biggest city in southern Bosnia and Herzegovina?

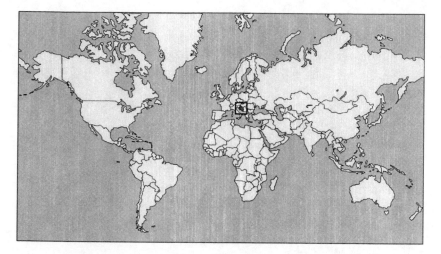

2. According to the 2008 census, what percentage of marriages in Mostar were mixed (Bosniak-Croat)?

3. According to the 2008 census, what percentage of marriages in Vukovar were mixed (Croat-Serb)?

For all the relaxed atmosphere, cool music and cheap beer, club Abrasevic in Mostar, a town in southwest Bosnia, is not just another alternative youth hangout.

As the main gathering place for the children of mixed marriages in Mostar, a city divided into Bosniak (Bosnian Muslim) and Croat sectors, the club is as infamous as the headquarters of a notorious sect might be.

"The only thing Croats and Muslims have in common is hatred for people in mixed marriages," says Nino Zelenika, 25, whose father is a Croat and whose mother is a Bosniak. "Both regard them as traitors."

The War

When war broke out in Bosnia and Herzegovina in 1992, Mostar's Bosniaks and Croats at first united to expel Bosnian Serb paramilitaries. However, the communities soon turned against one another and a bitter war-within-a-war erupted, lasting for a year.

At the time, Nino was only eight. Then mainly interested in Teenage Mutant Ninja Turtles and other cartoon heroes, he did not have the faintest idea who belonged to which nationality.

However, life soon taught him that nationality comes first and foremost in Mostar, and that different communities don't mix.

"People like us, living in mixed families, could only take the middle ground—and in the middle lies the river," Nino says bitterly, referring to the waters of the Neretva that flow through the city, separating the Muslim Bosniak east from the Catholic Croat west.

War Turns Love to Hate

After the disintegration of the multiethnic Yugoslav state, nationalist politicians played aggressively on people's national and religious feelings. Fear and a feeling of being under threat grew and people began isolating themselves within their respective ethnic camps.

Mostar, the biggest city in southern Bosnia and Herzegovina, was well known for its significant proportion of mixed marriages. The high level of ethnic mixing was perhaps unsurprising, as Mostar stood at the intersection of regions populated by Muslims, Croats and Serbs.

Vukovar, a small town on the easternmost edge of Croatia, boasted similar characteristics. Close to the border between Croatia and Serbia, Vukovar was another community in which there was a high degree of interethnic mingling.

As a result of their important geostrategic positions, both Mostar and Vukovar suffered appallingly in the wars of the early nineties. Vukovar was almost completely destroyed, while Mostar was significantly damaged. Many of their residents were wounded or killed. New, invisible ethnic divides separated the survivors.

While some local and international officials and media maintained that the level of destruction reflected the historic hatred between the different ethnic and religious groups in the Balkans, statistics concerning Mostar and Vukovar suggest that this thesis is incorrect.

Diverse and Tolerant Cities

In Vukovar, surveys from the 1990s reveal that some 23 ethnic groups then lived in the town. Mixed couples made up 34 per cent of all marriages. Recent surveys reported 97 per cent of Serbs claiming to have had close Croat friends, while 84 per cent of Croats said they had had close Serb friends.

Mostar was home to about 20 different ethnic groups and was widely seen as one of the most ethnically tolerant environments in the country.

"Ethnic intolerance was not a precursor to war, but its consequence," psychologist Dinka Corkalo Biruski, of Zagreb University, says. Her conclusion follows years of research into communities affected by war.

The views of American anthropologist Robert Hayden and sociologist Keith Doubt offer an explanation for the especially high level of violence experienced by Vukovar or Mostar, places where ethnic mixing was most pronounced.

"The more integrated the people are, the more violence is required to separate them," Doubt writes in his book *Sociology After Bosnia [and Kosovo]*.

Mostar was home to about 20 different ethnic groups and was widely seen as one of the most ethnically tolerant environments in the country.

Conflicts in the former Yugoslavia left both towns heavily scarred and ethnically separated. People in interethnic marriages and their offspring were left straddling new ethnic divides and facing hostility from both sides.

"People entering into mixed marriages today in cities like Vukovar and Mostar are heroes," Ljiljana Gehrecke, [from] . . . an NGO [nongovernmental organization] working on interethnic reconciliation in Vukovar, says.

"These are people with strong self-consciousness who have built a robust personal identity despite the pressure of the collective identity."

Mostar Wedding Procession Escorted by UN Peacekeepers

According to the 1991 census, 10 per cent of all marriages in Mostar were mixed. Nine years later, out of 176 marriages in Mostar, not one Bosniak-Croat couple spoke the words "I do". These two ethnic groups made up 47 and 48 per cent of Mostar's approximately 100,000 residents respectively.

A modest increase was recorded in 2004, when approximately 0.7 per cent of marriages were between Bosniak and Croat couples. In 2008, the figure was again slightly higher, at 1.6 per cent.

Husein Orucevic, a Bosniak, and Tanja Miletic Orucevic, a Croat, married in the devastated and divided Mostar of 1996. The situation was still so dangerous that wedding guests from the west of the city had to be escorted to the east in armoured UN [United Nations] peacekeeping vehicles.

"The path we chose was not easy," recalls Husein, the founder of the Abrasevic club. "We had to seek alternative jobs and find alternative places to meet our friends," he adds.

Mixed Marriage as Politically Subversive

Theatre director Tanja Miletic Orucevic believes the issue of mixed marriages is not publicly discussed in Mostar because such marriages are seen as a threat to the ruling nationalists.

"They've been preaching for almost two decades that the only way to survive is to stick to the flock," she says. "Whoever manages to live with someone from another flock undermines their concept."

Changing Demographics in Mostar and Vukovar

Mostar, Bosnia and Herzegovina:

1991—126,626 residents: 35% Bosniaks, 34% Croats, 19% Serbs

1992 to 1995—war, 2,532 dead: 62% Bosniaks, 19% Croats, 17% Serbs

2009—111,116 residents: 47% Bosniaks, 48% Croats, 3% Serbs

Vukovar, Croatia:

1991—44,639 residents: 47% Croats, 32% Serbs

1991 to 1998—war and Serbian occupation, 1,588 dead: 84% Croats, 7% Serbs

2009—31,670 residents: 58% Croats, 33% Serbs

TAKEN FROM: Barbara Matejcic, "Cruel Wars Cast Shadows over Mixed Marriages," Balkan Fellowship for Journalistic Excellence, 2009.

Alenka O, 34, a Bosniak woman from Mostar, says a mixed marriage in the city is never a private, personal affair. As the wife of a Croat, she says other Bosniaks view her as a traitor.

When the war broke out, she was 18, living with her mother and two younger sisters in the western, mainly Croat district. A Bosnian Croat soldier hid them in his apartment.

"We heard we were on some list and nothing good was happening to the people on the list: They were interned in camps, raped and murdered," she says.

"If it were not for him, a normal person in the midst of that madness, who knows what would've become of us?"

A year after the ordeal, the two were married.

A Tough Path

"Many a time I've regretted it because, although we get along fine, we don't belong anywhere," she says. Even the drastic act of conversion to Catholicism, Alenka feels, would not change the way in which she is regarded in the western side of town. In the east, her husband can expect similar treatment.

Their daughter, now 14, is a Croat, goes to a Croatian school and bears a Croatian surname. Alenka let her daughter be baptised, even though this was hard for her as a Muslim.

Although Alenka ponders why her child cannot take pride in her mixed background, ultimately, she already knows the answer. "I don't want my child to be of undefined nationality because I know what I've had to put up with," she says. "I'll probably live with this division until the end of my life, but I don't want her to live that way."

Finding Hope

A report published in July 2009 by leading international think tank the International Crisis Group, ICG, claims there is some hope that relations may ultimately normalise.

"The border between east and west Mostar is harder to spot these days but the city remains thoroughly divided, literally two cities, living side by side," the report says. "Even this represents progress: residents now cross safely and easily back and forth."

School Segregation

Meanwhile, some children growing up on different sides of the divide have no idea what the rest of the city looks like. Few mingle or date peers from the other ethnic group. They attend separate kindergartens, schools and universities.

The only significant kindergarten attended by children from both ethnic groups is financed by foreign funds and was originally meant for children with disabilities.

"The problem of school segregation is a major concern," says Caroline Ravaud, the head of the European Council in Bosnia.

Local and international experts say fear maintains ethnic divisions like those in Mostar: fear of leaving the mono-ethnic group; fear of being shunned by one's own ethno-religious group for mingling with others; fear over jobs and social security.

"When that fear fades away, a marriage between a Muslim and a Croat will become an issue of freedom of choice, and not a burden stemming that choice," says Mario Antonio Brkic, director of the Sarajevo Inter-Religious Institute.

"Then people will realise that mixed marriages are a societal category, testifying to the fact that they can live normally here irrespective of their differences," he adds.

Seeds of Potential Conflict in Vukovar

A few hundred kilometres to the north, in Vukovar, 34-year-old Srdan Sijakovic subscribes to the same idea.

"Take a Croat and a Serb in pre-war Vukovar and, if they were not religious, you would see no difference between their identities," says Sijakovic, the youngest Croat defender to have been on the infamous southern front line in 1991.

"Their alleged heterogeneity is imposed and politically constructed," he adds, raising his voice against the rumbling background of a band playing on a stage in the town's burnt-out baroque-style cultural centre. The building was destroyed by some of the 7,000 shells that besieging Serbs rained on Vukovar every day for three months in 1991.

Neither the cultural centre nor the prewar tolerance of Vukovar residents has been rebuilt to date. However, despite the terrible things that he witnessed on the battlefield, Sijakovic married a Serb woman, and the couple have a child now.

The two of them have no problems with one another, but others seem to have a problem with them, he says. For example, he might pay about 75 cents for a coffee in a Croat cafe, whereas his wife would be charged twice that amount. "National identity means that, if you're a Croat, then you hate Serbs, and vice versa," he says.

A Rare Occurrence

Despite a modest recent increase, Croat-Serb marriages like theirs remain rare. In 1998, they made up 5 per cent of all marriages in the town. In 2003 this figure was only 1.5 per cent and in 2008, 8 per cent.

"I don't know even today whether we were brave or just crazy," Vukovar resident Dijana Antunovic Lazic says of herself and her Serb husband, Sinisa. Both their parents were shocked when, in the middle of the war, they told them they intended to live together.

"They objected to our choice to live together with the enemy while 'our' people were dying every day," she recalls. "I think the biggest burden for them was what other people would say."

They married in 1994, during the third year of Serb rule in the town. "Those were difficult years. Many people didn't want to talk to us because they weren't thinking with their own heads, but as politics and the church instructed them," she adds.

A Changing Political Culture?

Things may be changing in Vukovar, however. Zeljko Sabo, elected in May 2009, is the first mayor since the war to have sprung from the ranks of moderate political option.

Politicians in the town encouraged a state of apartheid amongst Vukovar's children, from kindergartens to secondary schools, Sabo recalls. "You had to explain to a little child why it was impossible for him or her to go to the nearest kindergarten and why they had to go to another one," he says.

"At three, children learned who the Croats and who the Serbs were and, when parents lacked the patience to answer all the child's 'whys', then they cut it short and said, 'you can't go there because they slaughtered our people.'"

Ljiljana Gehrecke . . . says such attitudes have serious long-term consequences if they pass unchallenged.

"Not only does the segregation in Vukovar's schools make it impossible for kids to get to know one another and eventually marry across the ethnic divide, it also may lay the seeds of a future conflict," she warns.

Finding Peace Abroad

Many people from mixed Balkan marriages agree that, in such a divided ethnic environment, often, the only option left is to go abroad.

That is how Sanja Mihajlov, Hari Likic and their children Anej, Lina Lena and Timon Likic found the happiness that had eluded them at home.

Sanja is a Serb from Belgrade, while Hari is a Bosniak from Sarajevo. Destiny brought them together just before the war started in the coastal Croatian town of Sibenik, where Sanja was on vacation and Hari was serving in the Yugoslav navy.

They briefly settled in Sarajevo, but had to escape as Serb forces tightened their siege. They then travelled to Belgrade, but soon decided to move again.

"In Belgrade, when I saw our alcoholic neighbour cleaning his rifle before going to the war [in Croatia], it was clear we had to leave," Hari recalls. "It clearly depended on his mood whether he would point that rifle at me or not."

Many people from mixed Balkan marriages agree that, in such a divided ethnic environment, often, the only option left is to go abroad.

A Normal Life

In 1992, the couple left for the Netherlands and now live in the small town of Helmond. Lina Lena, who was born later that year, feels Dutch. If her parents belong to different ethnic groups from the former Yugoslavia, it is of no great relevance to her.

"A lot of people from all over the world are here, and no one cares where my parents are from and I couldn't care less either," the 17-year-old says.

Asked about his nationality, her brother, Timon, aged 14, is perplexed. He shrugs his shoulders and answers: "No one ever asked me that question before."

Nino Zelenika in Mostar was not so lucky. A child of a mixed Bosniak-Croat couple, aged eight when war broke out, he had to come up with an answer to this question by the time he was 14.

He is painfully aware that his identity is a combination of different ethnic and religious identities. "To reduce oneself to one's mere nationality would mean wasting one's life," he says, mentioning his plan to leave Mostar after graduation.

"I don't want to spend the next 40 years discussing who is a Croat and who is a Bosniak," he adds. "I need a normal life, and I don't see this happening, not now, not in the future."

Serbia's Surge in Mixed Marriages Is Reviving Dying Villages

Zoran Maksimovic

Zoran Maksimovic is a journalist. In the following viewpoint, he investigates the trend of Serbian bachelors marrying Albanian women in the southwest region of Serbia known as Sandzak. Maksimovic reports that the migration of young Serbian women in the area to larger cities to find employment has left a dearth of single women in Sandzak and a very low birth rate in many of the small villages in the region. The solution has been arranged marriages between these Serbian men and Albanian women from northern Albania, a region decimated by the migration of Albanian men to Greece to find employment. Although some are concerned that the influx of Albanian women to Sandzak will result in an "Albanianization" of the area, the majority of Serbians welcome these women as a way to revive and repopulate dying villages.

As you read, consider the following questions:

1. According to the author, how many Serb-Albanian marriages took place in the Sandzak region of Serbia between 2006–2008?

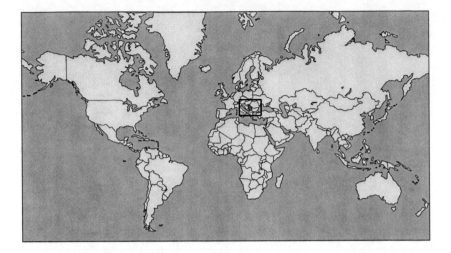

2. How many divorces have resulted from Albanian women marrying Serbian men for a "test period," according to Aferdita Crnisanin?

3. What humanitarian organization has taken an active matchmaking role for mixed couples?

The village of Budjevo, on the high Pester plains of Serbia's Sandzak region, is a desolate place, with winter temperatures plunging down as far as minus -40°C.

But the air of emptiness and abandonment may be changing at last. Little Milos Matovic, the first baby born in the village for many years, is now a year old, and Budjevo has welcomed several more children into its ranks in recent months.

A Growing Trend

There is nothing unusual, perhaps, in local bachelors getting married and starting families.

What is more unusual, given the traditional intolerance in the Balkans between Serbs and Albanians, is that several recent marriages in this village have been mixed, with Serbian grooms marrying Albanian brides.

The villagers insist that it doesn't matter that the brides come from northern Albania. The important thing is for local boys to get married and have children.

Little Milos is himself the fruit of one of these mixed marriages. His father, Radeta Matovic, is a well-known local Serb, while his mother, Vera, comes from a village in northern Albania, near Shkodër.

Vera is still learning Serbian, while Radeta has learned a few words in Albanian too.

Until recently, the only words Vera could say in Serbian were "fine" or "great" and she mainly communicated with her husband through hand gestures. Today, she speaks more fluently to her husband, though in Serbian that is still clumsy.

Though well aware that relations between Serbs and Albanians are usually poor, in this area, circumstances have forced people to think differently.

"Communicating is not a problem," says Radeta. "Vera has adjusted as if she was born here. Now we do all the chores around the house together."

Marriages like Radeta's and Vera's are becoming increasingly frequent in the remote corner of southwest Serbia known as the Sandzak, or Raska, region.

Apparently, about 80 such marriages have taken place in the last two years alone between Serbian bachelors and Albanian brides.

A Different Perspective

Though well aware that relations between Serbs and Albanians are usually poor, in this area, circumstances have forced people to think differently. Most local Serbs applaud the phenomenon, though a minority fear the practice of marrying Albanian women could lead to the area become "Albanianised".

Map of the Sandzak Region

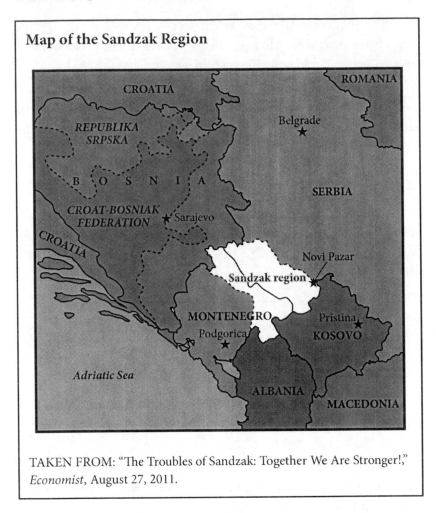

TAKEN FROM: "The Troubles of Sandzak: Together We Are Stronger!," *Economist*, August 27, 2011.

The stories of most of the grooms are similar. The local girls leave the villages to go to school then find jobs in the cities and stay there.

The boys, on the other hand, remain at home, obliged to help their parents, and eventually inheriting the pastures' herds. But the ageing parents of those men have only one wish, which is to see grandchildren and know their farms and households will not end up abandoned.

As for the Albanian girls, they, too, often lack suitable partners for marriage in their home district. Poverty forces most village boys around Shkodër to depart to work in Greece or other countries. They often marry there and remain abroad. That is how a similar fate has connected boys from southwest Serbia with girls from northern Albania.

Brides usually meet their future husbands in one of the villages near Shkoder. After, the parents of the brides-to-be go to check up on where their daughters will live.

Limited Choices

"The boys from our villages go to Greece to work and also get married there, so we don't really have a choice," one Albanian bride explained. "We want husbands, kids, and family harmony."

Aferdita Crnisanin, the only court interpreter in the Raska area who speaks Albanian, told *Balkan Insight* that she had attended the weddings of more than 20 such couples, mostly in the municipalities of Novi Pazar, Sjenica and Tutin.

Crnisanin admits that most of the brides do not speak a word of Serbian on their wedding day, but says that clearly does not represent an obstacle. "The good thing about it is that everyone is satisfied in these cases," she said.

A Test Period

She says some marriageable girls come to Serbia for a "test" period to live in their new home for a couple of months, and only then get married. According to her, there has not been a single divorce so far as a result of these mixed marriages, which speaks about the practice.

Radisa Savic, a Serb from Sopoćani, says his wife did not need a test run. His home yearned for a woman's touch, he says. He had lived with his father for years until an Albanian named Pamvera agreed to marry him. "She is so hard-working that I couldn't get on without her now," Savic said.

Much-Needed New Blood

Semiha Kacar, president of the Sandzak Committee for Protection of Human Rights, says the spate of local mixed marriages is helping to keep struggling villages alive.

"It's good that rural households do not fold, because the migration of the population from the villages to the cities is very pronounced," she said.

Kacar notes that women from villages in this part of Serbia have been marrying for centuries without knowing much about their future husbands. Such decisions were in the hands of family elders, so the fact that brides are marrying boys today that they barely know is nothing unusual.

Stara Raska: The Matchmaker

The idea to find wives for local bachelors was originally promoted by the humanitarian organization Stara Raska (Old Raska), which is based in Belgrade.

Mainly financed by the Serbian community in Canada, Stara Raska is trying to counter the effects of depopulation and the rural flight of Serbs from this part of the country.

"There are several thousand Serbian Orthodox bachelors aged between 25 and 45 in this region but 'the white plague' [contraception] is having dire consequences, primarily on the Orthodox population, changing the whole demographics in the Raska area," Vojin Vucicevic, the organisation's president, said.

"Stara Raska does not undertake a classic matchmaking role but . . . helps them," Vucicevic told *Balkan Insight*.

He said that in the beginning it had been very difficult to set up contacts between local bachelors and marriageable girls from further afield, but now it was easier, thanks to the help of the new Raska wives who have come from Albania.

Vucicevic said that his organisation was expanding its activities. "Having realised the importance of our role in assisting marriages in Sjenica, several months ago we founded the Association of Grooms from Stara Raska, which includes all the mixed marriages," he said.

"Members of this association will play a crucial role in the creation of new marriages."

Not everyone is delighted by the influx of Albanian wives, however. Some believe it will eventually mean the "Albanianisation" of the region.

Other Groups and Individuals

Milinko Rakonjac, from the village of Stavalj, was one of the first in these parts to marry an Albanian. He said he was persuaded to set off to a village near Shkodër by a woman who specialised in matchmaking.

Other groups and individuals, from clergy to local associations, are now also involved. "It is no secret that a priest from these parts is involved in matchmaking," one local groom who recently married a bride from Albania, said.

The same man said the Association of Serbs and Montenegrins in Albania, which has around 30,000 members in Ljes, Drac, Korça, Elbasan and Tirana, also plays a role in helping to fix up potential partners.

Criticisms

Not everyone is delighted by the influx of Albanian wives, however. Some believe it will eventually mean the "Albanianisation" of the region.

"These Albanian women who marry our people do not speak a word of Serbian and when they have children, their native tongue will be Albanian," one local complained.

But Stara Raska disagrees, adding that men from the Raska area have no other choice, and this way of choosing their life partner is quite acceptable if it prevents the death of family households.

"Claims about 'Albanianisation' are denied by the fact that these women give up Catholicism, take up Orthodoxy, marry in Orthodox churches and give their children Serbian names," Vucicevic said.

Mirko Popovac, a local journalist, agreed that fears of "Albanianisation" are exaggerated. "The phenomenon is not so widespread that it can endanger the national identity of this part of Serbia," he said.

He said it was commendable that marriageable girls wanted to live in the Serbian countryside and give birth to children there.

It is not a good thing if marriages are made without love, he went on. However, he added, the fact that most families speak highly of the experience proves that these marriages are working out.

Periodical and Internet Sources Bibliography

The following articles have been selected to supplement the diverse views presented in this chapter.

Radhika Holmstrom	"This Life: Radhika Holmstrom on Her Mixed-Race Heritage," *Daily Mail*, May 8, 2010.
Jerusalem Post	"Facing Intermarriage," March 15, 2010.
Francine Kiefer	"Egypt's Deadly Rumors of Interfaith Marriage," *Christian Science Monitor*, May 12, 2011.
Zerlina Maxwell	"Why Is There a Gender Gap for Blacks in Interracial Marriage?," The Grio, February 17, 2012.
Carol Morello	"Number of Biracial Babies Soars over Past Decade," *Washington Post*, April 26, 2012.
Ruben Navarrette	"Facing a Cultural Divide in My Mixed Marriage," CNN.com, July 7, 2011.
Alex Rodriguez	"Hindus in Pakistan Accuse Muslims of Kidnapping Teens as Wives," *Los Angeles Times*, April 22, 2012.
Andrea Stone	"Multiracial American Population Grew Faster than Single-Race Segment in 2010 Census," *Huffington Post*, September 27, 2012.
Taryam Al Subaihi	"The Truth on Mixed Marriages: Only the Strong Will Survive," *National* (United Arab Emirates), April 29, 2012.
Miriam Yuan	"Mixed Marriages in Singapore Give Hope for Baby Boom," *Bikya Masr* (Egypt), October 2, 2012.

For Further Discussion

Chapter 1

1. After reading the viewpoints in this chapter, what general trends do you see regarding interracial, interethnic, interfaith, and intercultural marriage? How accepting is your community to mixed marriage? Explain.

2. In Israel and Lebanon, interfaith couples cannot marry because the institution of marriage is controlled by religious authorities. In your opinion, should marriage be controlled by religious authorities? Provide support for your answer.

Chapter 2

1. What role does the media play in opposing or fostering acceptance of mixed marriage? In Rick Wallace's viewpoint, he asserts that Japanese media have made foreign men more appealing to Japanese women. How does the media influence the attitude toward interracial, interethnic, interfaith, and intercultural marriage in your community?

2. What factors explored in this chapter do you think are key in the reception and prevalence of mixed marriage? Explain why you think they are so important. Do these factors exist in your community? Explain.

Chapter 3

1. This chapter focuses on the barriers to mixed marriages in different parts of the world. What barriers to interracial, interethnic, interfaith, and intercultural marriage exist in your community? Which do not? Explain.

Chapter 4

1. In the first viewpoint of the chapter, Matthew Syed argues that with the number of mixed marriages increasing worldwide, many observers believe that racial distinctions will disappear. What do you think is the connection between the global prevalence of mixed marriage and racism? Explain your answer.

2. In Sultan Al Qassemi's viewpoint, he contends that mixed marriage is a benefit for the United Arab Emirates. Do you agree or disagree with this assessment? Provide an explanation for your answer.

Organizations to Contact

The editors have compiled the following list of organizations concerned with the issues debated in this book. The descriptions are derived from materials provided by the organizations. All have publications or information available for interested readers. The list was compiled on the date of publication of the present volume; the information provided here may change. Be aware that many organizations take several weeks or longer to respond to inquiries, so allow as much time as possible.

American Civil Liberties Union (ACLU)
125 Broad Street, 18th Floor, New York, NY   10004
(888) 567-ACLU
website: www.aclu.org

The American Civil Liberties Union (ACLU) is a national organization that works to protect the rights of individuals and communities as prescribed by the US Constitution. The ACLU lobbies Congress to pass legislation protecting civil liberties; employs lawyers to fight discrimination and injustice in court; and organizes activists, volunteers, and other organizations to protest the violation of civil liberties. The ACLU website features a blog, called *The Blog of Rights*, which offers opinions and commentary from staff and legal scholars on hot topics and current campaigns and cases. The website also provides video of interviews, commentary, and presentations on ACLU efforts on subjects such as immigration and same-sex marriage.

Association of MultiEthnic Americans (AMEA)
PO Box 341304, Los Angeles, CA   90034
(877) 954-AMEA
e-mail: info@ameasite.org
website: www.ameasite.org

The Association of MultiEthnic Americans (AMEA) is an independent organization that was formed to promote the interests of and to give a voice to the multiethnic, multiracial, and transnational community. AMEA also facilitates collaboration between organizations dedicated to multiethnic, multiracial, and transracial adoptee issues. Most of the group's activities are at the local level, where the AMEA brings together members for cultural and social events. It also works with academics and professionals to explore issues of interest. The AMEA is a resource for the community and provides information on health and legal topics, breaking news, a recommended reading list, and access to the AMEA newsletter.

Center for Economic and Social Rights (CESR)
162 Montague Street, 3rd Floor, Brooklyn, NY 11201
(718) 237-9145 • fax: (718) 237-9147
e-mail: info@cesr.org
website: www.cesr.org

The Center for Economic and Social Rights (CESR) is an international organization that promotes social justice through human rights. CESR describes its mission as such: "In a world where poverty and inequality deprive entire communities of dignity, justice, and sometimes life, we seek to uphold the universal human rights of every human being to education, health, food, water, housing, work, and other economic, social and cultural rights essential to human dignity." In recent years, CESR has been developing new ways to measure and monitor economic and social rights compliance. The CESR website features a blog examining current human rights issues and CESR events. It also provides country fact sheets, in-depth studies on social rights issues, and other resources.

Human Rights First
333 Seventh Avenue, 13th Floor, New York, NY 10001
(212) 845-5200 • fax: (212) 845-5299
e-mail: feedback@humanrightsfirst.org
website: www.humanrightsfirst.org

Human Rights First is an independent international organization that advances human rights through accurate research and reporting on human rights abuses worldwide, advocacy for victims, and coordination with other organizations. The group is focused in five key areas: crimes against humanity, fighting discrimination, aiding human rights activists, refugee protection, and advocating for fair legal protections. To that end, Human Rights First offers a series of in-depth studies on such issues, including recent reports on anti-Semitism in Europe, oppressive government counterterrorist measures in Uzbekistan, and China's role in the Sudanese conflict. It also provides an e-newsletter, *Rights Wire*, which examines issues in the human rights field.

Institute on Religion and Public Policy

500 North Washington Street, Alexandria, VA   22314
(703) 888-1700 • fax: (703) 888-1704
website: religionandpolicy.org

The Institute on Religion and Public Policy is an international nonpartisan organization that works to protect the practice of religious freedom around the world. To that end, it researches and disseminates information and analysis on oppressive governments and policies that threaten that freedom. The institute also sponsors programs and events to educate and motivate activists, government policy makers, academics, business executives, religious leaders, and nongovernmental organizations. It publishes a weekly newsletter, *Face of Freedom*, which offers analysis on the state of global religious freedom. In addition, the institute's website also features a blog focusing on current issues and events.

Interfaith Family (IFF)

90 Oak Street, 4th Floor, PO Box 428
Newton Upper Falls, MA   02464
(617) 581-6860 • fax: (617) 965-7772
website: www.interfaithfamily.com

Interfaith Family (IFF) is a comprehensive resource for interfaith families exploring Jewish life and inclusive Jewish communities. IFF connects individuals, families, and communities with Jewish welcoming committees as well as religious and professional services. It also offers a wide range of educational materials for partners in interfaith relationships and marriages. IFF's online resources include guides for interfaith families; articles, essays, and discussions about the unique issues interfaith families face; referrals to clergy, synagogues, and other Jewish organizations; and information on events around the country for interfaith couples.

International Partnership for Human Rights (IPHR)

Avenue des Arts 3-4-5, 8th Floor, Brussels   1210
  Belgium
+32 2 227 6145
e-mail: IPHR@IPHRonline.org
website: www.iphronline.org

The International Partnership for Human Rights (IPHR) is a nonprofit organization consisting of practitioners and activists dedicated to promoting human rights around the world. IPHR researches and reports on human rights abuses and governmental compliance with human rights obligations; coordinates policy on the issue with international organizations, nongovernmental groups, and local activists; and develops and implements projects that advance the global state of human rights. The IPHR website features access to various reports, studies, letters, press releases, and news articles on relevant topics.

Jewish Outreach Institute (JOI)

1270 Broadway, Suite 609, New York, NY   10001
(212) 760-1440 • fax: (212) 760-1569
e-mail: info@joi.org
website: joi.org

The Jewish Outreach Institute (JOI) is "an independent, national, trans-denominational organization reaching out to unaffiliated and intermarried families." JOI was created in 1987 to formulate innovative programs, conduct research, and provide training to Jewish professionals and volunteers working in outreach programs all over the country. One of its programs is the Mothers Circle, which provides access to free resources, education, and events for women of other religious backgrounds raising Jewish children. The JOI website lists upcoming events and links to the *JOI Newsletter*, as well as catalogues a number of recommended books and reading material. There is also a library of recent JOI research on intermarriage and other related topics.

United Nations Human Rights Council

Palais des Nations, Geneva 10   CH-1211
  Switzerland
+41 22 917 9220
e-mail: InfoDesk@ohchr.org
website: www.ohchr.org

The Human Rights Council is a part of the United Nations that focuses on strengthening and protecting human rights around the globe. The council is tasked with making recommendations on some of the most pressing human rights situations worldwide. It works closely with other bodies in the United Nations as well as with national and local governments, nongovernmental organizations, and human rights activists. Transcripts and videos of the council's sessions can be found on the group's website, which also features current news and information on recent reports and proceedings.

US Department of Health and Human Services (HHS)

200 Independence Avenue SW, Washington, DC   20201
(877) 696-6775
website: www.hhs.gov

The Department of Health and Human Services (HHS) is the US agency tasked with protecting the health of all Americans. The HHS oversees the Administration for Children and Families (ACF), a department that manages and develops programs that touch on welfare, child welfare, child support enforcement, foster care, adoption assistance, and child abuse. The ACF is focused on empowering families and individuals to achieve economic independence; providing services to the poor, neglected, refugees, and disabled; and fostering strong, robust, and safe communities. The HHS and ACF websites offer fact sheets, reports, manuals, and issue briefs as well as other publications to help American families and individuals.

Bibliography of Books

Paul R. Amato, Alan Booth, David R. Johnson, and Stacy J. Rogers
Alone Together: How Marriage in America Is Changing. Cambridge, MA: Harvard University Press, 2007.

Fay Botham
Almighty God Created the Races: Christianity, Interracial Marriage & American Law. Chapel Hill: University of North Carolina Press, 2009.

Jill M. Bystydzienski
Intercultural Couples: Crossing Boundaries, Negotiating Difference. New York: New York University Press, 2011.

Michael O. Emerson and George Yancey
Transcending Racial Barriers: Toward a Mutual Obligations Approach. New York: Oxford University Press, 2011.

W. Ralph Eubanks
The House at the End of the Road: The Story of Three Generations of an Interracial Family in the American South. New York: Smithsonian Books, 2009.

Diane Farr
Kissing Outside the Lines: A True Story of Love and Race and Happily Ever After. Berkeley, CA: Seal Press, 2011.

Cheryl Judice
Interracial Marriages Between Black Women and White Men. Amherst, NY: Cambria Press, 2008.

Christelyn D. Karazin and Janice Rhoshalle Littlejohn — *Swirling: How to Date, Mate, and Relate Mixing Race, Culture, and Creed*. New York: Atria Paperback, 2012.

Terri A. Karis and Kyle D. Killian, eds. — *Intercultural Couples: Exploring Diversity in Intimate Relationships*. New York: Brunner-Routledge, 2008.

Mary Ann Lamanna and Agnes Riedmann — *Marriages, Families, and Relationships: Making Choices in a Diverse Society*. 11th ed. Belmont, CA: Cengage Learning/Wadsworth, 2012.

Kevin Noble Maillard and Rose Cuison Villazor, eds. — *Loving v. Virginia in a Post-Racial World: Rethinking Race, Sex, and Marriage*. New York: Cambridge University Press, 2012.

Keren R. McGinity — *Still Jewish: A History of Women and Intermarriage in America*. New York: New York University Press, 2009.

Phyl Newbeck — *Virginia Hasn't Always Been for Lovers: Interracial Marriage Bans and the Case of Richard and Mildred Loving*. Carbondale: Southern Illinois University Press, 2004.

Peggy Pascoe — *What Comes Naturally: Miscegenation Law and the Making of Race in America*. New York: Oxford University Press, 2009.

Naomi Schaefer Riley — *'Til Faith Do Us Part: How Interfaith Marriage Is Transforming America*. New York: Oxford University Press, 2013.

Dugan Romano   *Intercultural Marriage: Promises and Pitfalls.* 3rd ed. Boston, MA: Intercultural Press, 2008.

Michael J. Rosenfeld   *The Age of Independence: Interracial Unions, Same-Sex Unions, and the Changing American Family.* Cambridge, MA: Harvard University Press, 2007.

Erika B. Seamon   *Interfaith Marriage in America: The Transformation of Religion and Christianity.* New York: Palgrave Macmillan, 2012.

Earl Smith and Angela J. Hattery, eds.   *Interracial Relationships in the 21st Century.* 2nd ed. Durham, NC: Carolina Academic Press, 2012.

Bryan Strong and Theodore F. Cohen   *The Marriage and Family Experience: Intimate Relationships in a Changing Society.* 12th ed. Belmont, CA: Cengage Learning/Wadsworth, 2014.

George Yancey   *Interracial Contact and Social Change.* Boulder, CO: Lynne Rienner Publishers, 2007.

Index

Geographic headings and page numbers in **boldface** refer to viewpoints about that country or region.

A

Abdullah, Basil, 62
Abdul-Sater, Joseph, 61
Acceptance of mixed marriage
    Bosnia and Herzegovina, 189
    Canada, 64–69
    Cyprus, 58–61
    England, 34, 37–40, 54–55
    Kuwait, 177–179
    Malaysia, 75–77
    North America, 42–43, 45
    Serbia, 198–201
    United States, 26–30
Adoyo, Everlyn, 132, 133, 134–135
Africa, 136–140
    intertribal marriage, 136–140
    Kenyan tribal culture, 131–135, 139
African Americans
    anti-miscegenation laws, 17–18, 25, 38, 161
    demographics, 29
    interracial marriages, 28–31, 37–38
    racial attitudes in US, 25
Afrida, Nani, 93–98
Afro-Turk population
    demographics, 171
    interracial marriages, 173
    preserving culture, 169–172, 175
    racial attitudes, 173–174
Age groups, 89–90, 89t
Ah Foo, Emily, 37
Al Haddad, Ahmed, 182–183

Al Mubarak, Razan, 183
Al Otaiba, Yousef, 183
Alabama, Pace v. (1883), 18
Alagiah, George, 32–40
Albanian-Serbian mixed marriages, 198–204
"All for Civil Marriage in Lebanon" campaign, 62
Al-Sayegh, Wael, 184
Amante, Maragtas S.V., 155
Anggraini, Rulita, 96
Anser, Layachi, 178
Anti-miscegenation laws, 17–18, 25, 38, 161
Arranged marriages, 16, 177–178
Asian American mixed marriages, 26, 27–28, 29–30, 163
    See also South Asians, North American
Associated Press, 57–62
Atheism, 123
Attractiveness of mixed-race people, 34, 166

B

Balta, Mohammed Dali, 61
Bangladeshi mixed marriages, 39, 163
Barriers to mixed marriage
    anti-miscegenation laws, 17–18, 25, 38, 161
    cultural bias, 43–44
    fear of cultural dilution, 53–54

gender expectations, 45–48

generational expectations, 53–54, 55, 113, 114–115

lack of cultural integration, 153–157

legal discrimination, 37, 117–120

organized opposition, 55–56

sectarian tensions, 122–125, 127–130

socioeconomic discrimination, 112

stigma, 122–123, 137–140

tribal fighting, 132–135

See also Racial prejudice; Religious pressure

Bedi, Pooja, 110–111, 115

Bengali, Shashank, 131–135

Betrayal, in inter-tribal conflicts, 138–139

BharatMatrimony.com, 42

Biruski, Dinka Corkalo, 189

Boateng, Paul, 162

Bollywood, 111–112

Borowiec, Steven, 152–157

Bosnia and Herzegovina, 121–130, 186–196

establishment, 126

mixed couples face ethnic discrimination, 186–196

Mostar demographics, 191

sectarian divide and interfaith marriage, 121–130

war, 187–188

Breeding Between the Lines (Ziv), 167

British National Party (BNP), 55–56

Brkic, Mario Antonio, 192–193

"Brown babies," 38

Budjevo, Serbia, 198

Business and diversity, 67–68

C

California, 19

Canada

diversity, 64–68

history, 65–67

Toronto as mixed marriage capital, 63–69

Caribbean mixed marriages, 39, 40, 163

Caste system, India, 112

Catholic-Protestant marriage, Northern Ireland, 85–92

Catholic-Protestant relations, Northern Ireland, 86–87, 91–92

Caucasian populations. *See* White populations

Chakravarty, Subrata, 48–50

Chaudhry, Rajive, 47–48, 50–51

Children of mixed marriages

demographics, 34, 39, 40

ethnic identity, 149–151, 191–192, 196

impact on race relations, 26–27

legal issues, 17, 25, 95–97, 117–120

living abroad, 195–196

measurement, 35

racial prejudice, 36, 37, 123, 157, 187

religious conversion, 103, 146

school issues, 124–125, 192, 194

success, 156, 162

Chinese mixed marriages

Canada, 66–67

England, 39

Korea, 155

Christians

Christianity in Philippines, 100–101

culture, 101–102, 105–106

intermarriage in England, 39
See also Muslim-Christian mixed marriages
Chui, Tina, 66
Citizenship law, Indonesia, 96
City of Life (film), 183
Civil marriages, Middle East rejection, 58, 59–61, 62
Civil rights movement, 19
The Cleanest Race (Myers), 157
Cojuangco, Tingting, 99–107
Common-law marriages, 62
Conrad, Lisa, 176–180
Consequences of mixed marriage
  blurred racial distinctions, 163–167
  contributions of mixed-race people, 44, 114–115, 183–185
  decreased racism, 166
  discrimination, 173–175
  ethnic identity issues, 149–151, 191–192, 196
  healthy marriages, 43, 51, 177 178
  imprisonment, 161
  living abroad, 195–196
  loss of rights, 37, 95–98, 117–119
  political undertones, 190–191
  racial prejudice, 36, 123–124, 187, 194
  reviving dying villages, 198–204
Contact hypothesis, 86
Contraception, 202
Crnisanin, Aferdita, 201
Croatia, 186–196
  barriers to mixed marriages, 186–196
  Croat-Serb marriages, 193–194
Cultural bias, 43–44, 46–47

Cultural identity
  Afro-Turks, 169–172, 175
  Russians, 143, 147
  South Asians, 43–44, 53–54
Cultural integration
  South Korea, 156, 157
  United Kingdom, 163
Cultural pressure in Russia, 143–144
Cyprus, 57–62
  history, 60
  interfaith marriages, 57–62

D

Dana Bayrami, 169–170, 175
Darangen, 101–102
Davdiev, Zaur, 144
Desai-Khan, Anu, 110
Discrimination, legal
  England, 37
  Jordan, 117–120
  United States, 17–18, 25, 38, 161
Discrimination, racial
  Bosnia and Herzegovina, 123, 124, 187, 194
  South Asians in North America, 50–51
  See also Racial prejudice
Discrimination, socioeconomic, 112
Diversity
  Canada, 64–68
  Malaysia, 74, 76–77
  United Arab Emirates, 184–185
  United States, 28
Divorce rates in Kuwaiti mixed marriages, 177, 178
Dizdarević, Damir, 121–130
Dnevni Avaz (newspaper), 123–124

Doubt, Keith, 189
Dual citizenship, Indonesia, 96,
  97–98
Dutt, Sanjay, 112

E

Education
    Afro-Turks, 171
    Bosnia and Herzegovina, 124–
      125, 192, 194
    Jordan, 118
    Northern Ireland, 89–91
    South Korea, 156
Eid al-Fitr, 36
Emiratis, prominent, 183–184
England, 32–40, 52–56
    demographics, 34, 36*t*, 39–40
    legal discrimination, 37
    mixed marriages are common,
      32–40
    organized opposition to
      mixed marriage, 55–56
    racial attitudes, 34–40
    South Asian mixed marriages,
      52–56
English-Yemeni relationships,
  35–37
Ethnic identity
    Bosnia and Herzegovina, 191–
      192, 196
    Russia, 143, 149–151
Euan-Smith, Roz, 52–56
Eugenics, 35

F

Fear, and ethnic segregation, 192–
  193
Fear of cultural dilution, 53–54
Feminism, 37
Fourteenth Amendment, 19, 28
Fryer, Roland, 162

G

Gaisen, 79
Gay marriage, 49, 61, 65
Gehrecke, Ljiljana, 190, 194
Gender issues
    British Asians, 55
    India, 45–48
    Indonesia, 95–98
    Japan, 80–81, 83–84
    Jordan, 117–120
    Kuwait, 178–179, 180
    Russia, 149
    Serbia, 200–201, 202
    See also Men in mixed mar-
      riages; Women in mixed
      marriages
Generational expectations
    Indian, 42, 113, 114–115
    South Asian, 44, 53–54, 55
Genetics, similarity among races,
  164
Ghamloush, Nada, 58, 59, 62
Ghobash, Omar Saif, 183
Ghosh, Srilata, 115
Gladwell, Malcolm, 162
Goli, Srinivas, 112
Guess Who's Coming to Dinner
  (film), 161–162

H

Habashney, Nima, 117, 118–119
Haddad, Ahmed Al, 182–183
Hamilton, Lewis, 34, 162
Harpending, Henry, 165
Harvard Implicit Association Test,
  165
Hayden, Robert, 189
Health, mixed marriages
    factors affecting, 74
    Indian, 113

Kuwaiti, 177–178
North American South Asians, 43, 48–49, 51
Health, mixed-race people, 166–167
Herzegovina. *See* Bosnia and Herzegovina
Hindu Code Bill, 113
Hindus, 39, 45–46
Hirji, Zabeen, 67–68
Hispanic American mixed marriages, 26, 27–28, 29
History of intermarriage
    global, 24–25
    United States, 16–19, *27*
Ho, Connie, 34–35
Human Genome Project, 164
"Hybrid vigor," 34, 167

I

Immigration law, Indonesian, 96
Inbreeding, 167
India, 109–115
    fear of cultural dilution, 43–44, 45, 53–54
    gender expectations, 45–48
    generational expectations, 113, 114–115
    intercaste marriage, 112
    mixed marriages, 109–115
Indian mixed marriages abroad, 39, 43, 44–46
Indonesia, 93–98
Indonesian Mixed Marriage Society (PerCa), 96
Inman, Arpana, 42–43, 51
Integration
    cultural, 156, 157, 163
    racial, 165

Interfaith marriage
    Bosnia and Herzegovina, 122–130
    England, 39
    India, 110–115
    Middle East, 58–62
    Northern Ireland, 86–92
    Philippines, 100–106
    Russia, 142–151
Internet
    Indonesian law research, 94, 95
    Russian mixed-marriage discussions, 144–145
Interracial marriage
    Afro-Turk population, 173
    England, 33–40, *36t*
    India, 112
    reactions, 137–138
    United States, 16–19, 24–31, *27*
Intertribal marriage, 132–135, 138–140
Ireland. *See* Northern Ireland
Islam
    Bosnia and Herzegovina, 123–125
    Philippines, 100, 101, 103
Israel, 58, 59–61, 62
Izmir, Turkey, 172

J

Jain, Shobha, 113
Japan, 78–84
    cultural influence, 82
    gender issues, 80–82, 83–84
    media influence, 79–80
    mixed marriages, 78–84
Jewish mixed marriages, 39
Jones, Steve, 164
Jordan, 116–120

K

Kabungsuan, Sharif, 100, 101, 104, 105

Kacar, Semiha, 202

Kaier, Maureen, 36–37

Kaier, Norman, 36–37

Karabat, Ayse, 168–175

Karadzic, Radovan, 126

Karanja, Josphat, 132, 133, 134

Kartmazova, Irina, 145

Kayacan, Gülay, 170–171

Kenya, 131–135

    demographics, 134*t*

    election controversy, 133–134

    tribal fighting frightens mixed couples, 131–135

Khan, Aamir, 111

Khan, Arbaaz, 111

Khan, Rukh, 111

Khan, Salman, 111

Khan, Zaheer, 114

Khan, Zayed, 111

Kibaki, Mwai, 132, 133

Kikuyus, 133, 134, 135

Kim Hee-kyung, 156

King, Andrew, 18

KITAP (permanent-stay permits), 96, 97

KITAS (temporary-stay permits), 96, 97

Konaçer, Emine, 172

Konaçer, Mehmet, 172–173

Koran, 103

Korneva, Lidia, 142, 149

Kurayev, Andrei, 146

Kuwait, 176–180

L

Label judgments, 165

Lazic, Dijana Antunovic, 194

Lebanon, 58, 59, 61, 62

Lee Chan-boum, 157

Legal issues in Indonesian mixed marriages, 94–98

Lepeska, David, 41–51

Lichter, Daniel, 26–27

Likic, Hari, 195

Lloyd, Katrina, 85–92

Love Will Follow (Sandhya), 43

Loving v. Virginia (1967), 19, *27*, 28

Luos, 133, 134–135

M

Maheux, Hélène, 66

Maksimovic, Zoran, 197–204

Malaysia, 72–77

    diversity, 74, 75, 76–77

    mixed marriages, 72–77

Maranao ancestry, 105

Marriage, religious meanings, 61

Marriage brokers, for-profit, 153–154, 155–156

Martin, Tony, 38

Maryland, 17

Maryoto Sumadi, 97

Massachusetts, 18

Matchmaking, 202–203

Matejcic, Barbara, 186–196

Mayasari, Renny, 94

McClinch, Janis, 47, 50–51

McKaiser, Eusebius, 25–26

Media influence, 79–80

Mehta, Zubin, 44

Men in mixed marriages

    English, 29

Filipino, 101, 102, 103–104
Japanese, 81
Jordanian, 117
Russian, 144–145
South Asian, 43, 45–46, 46
South Korean, 155
Men's attitudes about mixed marriages
British Asian, 55
Japanese, 83–84
Middle East, mixed marriage in, 58, 61, 62
Mihajlov, Sanja, 195
Milan, Anne, 66
Milosevic, Slobodan, 126
Miscegenation, 17–18, 25, 38, 161
Mississippi Black Code, 17
Mixed Britannia (documentary), 34, 38
Mixed-race people
acceptance, 26–27
attractiveness, 34, 167
categorizing, 68
England, 34, 36–37, 39
health, 166–167
United States, 28, 29
See also children
Mokarrab, Waleed Al, 183–184
Moro women, 101, 102
Mostafa, Ali, 183
Mostar, Bosnia and Herzegovina, 188–189, 190–191
Mubarak, Razan Al, 183
Mukhametshin, Rafik, 147, 148
Murad, Nermeen, 119
Murder, 153
Muslim culture, 101–102, 105–106
Muslim-Christian mixed marriages
Bosnia and Herzegovina, 191
England, 39

Philippines, 103–104
Russia, 142–149
Myers, Brian, 157

N

Nairobi, 133, 135
Najib Tun Razak, Datuk, 75–76
Nguyen Ngoc Cam, 154
NIMMA (Northern Ireland Mixed Marriage Association), 87
North America, 41–51
barriers to South Asian mixed marriage, 43–44, 49–51
South Asian mixed marriages, 41–51
South Asians gender expectations, 45–48
Northern Ireland, 85–92
Catholic-Protestant relations, 86–87
demographics, 88–91, 89t
mixed-religion marriage, 85–92
political affiliations, 90–92
Northern Ireland Life and Times (NILT) Survey, 87–88
Northern Ireland Mixed Marriage Association (NIMMA), 87

O

Obama, Barack, 29, 30, 162
Obeiya, Abdo, 35
Olpak, Mustafa, 170, 174, 175
"One drop" rule, 25
Ongkili, Maximus, 76
Orucevic, Husein, 190
Orucevic, Tanja Miletic, 190
Otaiba, Yousef Al, 183
Ozongwu, Melinda, 136–140

P

Pace v. Alabama (1883), 18
Pachauri, Manda, 111
Pakistanis, 39, 167
Palestine-Jordan relations, 120
Pankhurst, Alex, 82, 83
Pankhurst, Ayano, 82
Parekh, Malaika, 111
Parents. *See* Generational expectations
Patel, Anil, 53–54
Patil, Vimla, 109–115
Pennsylvania, 18
PerCa (Indonesian Mixed Marriage Society), 96
Perez v. Sharp, 18–19
Permanent-stay permits (KITAP), 96, 97
Philippines, 99–106
    interfaith marriages, 99–106
    religious culture, 101–103, 105–106
    Royal Noni legend, 104–105
Political affiliation, Northern Ireland, 90–92
Political implications of interracial marriage, 30–31
Polygamy, 101–102
Popovac, Mirko, 204
Portugal, 100–101
Prejudice. *See* Racial prejudice
Prenuptial agreements, 94, 95
Prevalence of mixed marriage, factors affecting
    acceptance, 76
    cultural diversity, 74, 75, 76–77
    cultural integration, 86–87, 90–91
    heritage, 105–106
    legal context, 94–98
    lure of the exotic, 84
    media influence, 79–80
    practical advantages, 82–83
    racial attitudes, 26–28
    socioeconomic factors, 88–90
Protestant-Catholic marriage, Northern Ireland, 85–92
Protestant-Catholic relations, Northern Ireland, 86–87, 91–92
Psychology and race, 165

Q

Qassemi, Sultan Al, 181–185
Qur'an, 103

R

Race
    genetic similarity, 164–165
    psychology and, 165
Racial discrimination
    Bosnia and Herzegovina, 123, 124, 187, 194
    South Asian North American mixed marriages, 50–51
    See also Discrimination, legal
Racial distinctions, blurring, 161–167
Racial integration, 165
Racial prejudice
    Bosnia and Herzegovina, 123–125
    Canada, 66–67
    Croatia, 194
    effect of integration on, 86, 165
    England, 36–38
    North America, 49–51
    South Asian North American mixed marriages, 49–51
    South Korea, 157
    Tamil Brahmins, 43–44, 46–47

Turkey, 173–174
United States, 17, 25, 161–162
Rais Yatim, 73–74
Rajah, M., 72–77
Rakonjac, Milinko, 203
Rania, Queen, 119
Ravaud, Caroline, 192
Reed, Imogen, 81
Religious conversion, 144, 145,
146–147, 149
Religious pressure
Bosnia and Herzegovina, 124–
125, 127–128
Middle East, 58, 61
Russia, 144–147
Reputation in Kuwaiti marriages,
179–180
Robinson, Gillian, 85–92
Rosenblum, Irit, 62
Royal Bank of Canada (RBC),
67–68
Royal Noni legend, 104–105
Russia, 141–151
dialogue, 144–148
ethnic identity, 149–151
history, 143–144
mixed marriages endangered,
141–151
traditional values, 148–149

S

Sabah, Malaysia, 75, 76
Sabo, Zeljko, 194
Salakhetdinov, Erkin, 150
Same-sex marriage, 49, 61, 65
Sampiano, Quirino, 104
Sandhya, Shaifali, 43, 45–46
Sandzak region, 198, *200*, 202
Sarajevo, Bosnia and Herzegovina,
122–125, 127–130
Sarawak, Malaysia, 75–76

Savic, Radisa, 201
Sayegh, Wael Al-, 184
Schools
mixed-religion, 90–91
political controversy, 124–125
segregated, 192
SDS (Serbian Democratic Party),
126
Serb-Croat marriages, 193–194
Serbia, 197–204
"Albanianisation" of region,
203–204
mixed marriages surge, 197–
204
Serbian Democratic Party (SDS),
126
Sharma, Richa, 112
Sharp, Perez v., 18–19
Sharvani, Isha, 114
Shaw, Sarah, 184
Shores of Slaves, The (Olpak), 175
Sijakovic, Srdan, 193
Sikhs, 39
Simpson, Ludi, 166
Singh, Deepti, 112
Slave Woman Kemale (Olpak), 175
Slavery
Turkey, 170–171, 175
United States, 17, 18
Smith, Zadie, 34, 162
Socio-economic issues in mixed
marriages
Africa, 139
Northern Ireland, 88–89, 89*t*,
91
South Korea, 154–155, 156
Sociology After Bosnia (Doubt),
189
Sökmen, Melis, 170
Soni, Jimmy, 45

South Africa, racial attitudes in, 25–26

South Asians, Bangladeshi, 39, 163

South Asians, British, 39, 53–56

South Asians, North American
  barriers to mixed marriage, 43–44, 49–51
  gender expectations, 45–48
  mixed marriages, 42–51

South Korea, 152–157
  marriage brokers, 153–154, 155
  multicultural marriages not supported, 152–157

South Pacific (musical), 104

Sözer, Ayse, 173–174

Spain, 100–101

Spector, J. Brooks, 23–31

Srebrenica, 125

Stafeev, Dimitri, 58, 59–61, 62

Stara Raska, 202–203

Stigmas, mixed marriage
  Africa, 137–140
  Bosnia and Herzegovina, 122–123

Stolyarova, Guzel, 144, 148, 149

Suljagic, Emir, 124–125, 127

Sultanate, 103

Syed, Matthew, 160–167

Sysoev, Daniel, 145–146

T

Taib Mahmud, 76

Talwar, Ankit, 114

Tamil Brahmins, 43–44, 46–47

Tatarstan, 148

Taylor, Paul, 30

Temporary-stay permits (KITAS), 96, 97

Thirteenth Amendment, 18

Tishkov, Valery, 143

Tito, Josip Broz, 124, 126

Toronto, Ontario, 63–69

Transjordanians, 119

Treaty of Tordesillas, 100

Tribal conflict, Kenya, 132–135

Turkey, 168–175
  Afro-Turk population, 168–175
  Izmir, 172
  racial misconceptions, 173–174

U

United Arab Emirates (UAE), 181–185
  diversity, 184–185
  mixed marriage benefits, 181–185
  mixed marriage controversy, 182–183

United Kingdom, 163
  See also England

United States, 23–31
  anti-miscegenation laws, 17–18, 25, 38, 161
  demographics, 27–30, 162–163
  interracial marriage, 23–31
  legal context, 19, *27*, 28, 161
  political implications of interracial marriage, 30–31
  racial attitudes, 25, 26–27, 161–162

Uys, Pieter-Dirk, 26

V

Values of South Asian North Americans, 44, 45

Vermont, 28

Vietnamese mixed marriages, 155

Virginia, 17, 18, 30–31

Virginia, Loving v. (1967), 19, *27*, 28

Voices Coming from a Silent Past (oral history), 171
Vucicevic, Vojin, 202–203, 204
Vukovar, Croatia, 188–189, 191, 193, 194

W

Wadia, Roy, 49
Wakim, Elie, 58, 59, 62
Wallace, Rick, 78–84
Warren, Earl, 19
White populations
    intermarriage in England, 39
    intermarriage in US, 28, 29–30
Women in mixed marriages
    English, 39
    Filipino, 101–102, 103–104
    Indian North American, 43, 46–47
    Japanese, 79–84
    Russian, 144
    South Asian North American, 46
    South Korean, 155
Women's rights
    Indonesia, 95–98

Jordanian mixed marriages, 117–120
Wong, Jan, 63–70
Woods, Tiger, 162

Y

Yamamoto, Beverley, 79–80, 83
Yemeni-English relationships, 35–37
Yugoslavia
    establishment of Bosnia and Herzegovina, 126
    mixed marriage, 122, 123
Yugoslavia, former
    Croatia, 188–189, 191, 193, 194
    See also Bosnia and Herzegovina
Yükseker, Deniz, 169–170
Yürür, Ahmet, 174–175

Z

Zaytseva, Olga, 58, 59–61
Zecchini, Laurent, 116–120
Zelenika, Nino, 187, 188, 196
Ziv, Alon, 167
Zolotov, Andrei, 141–151

CPSIA information can be obtained
at www.ICGtesting.com
Printed in the USA
FFOW05n0015280214